NARCISSISM HAS NO FACE

SUE BARKER

BALBOA.PRESS

A DIVISION OF HAY HOUSE

Balboa Press books may be ordered through booksellers or by contacting:

Balboa Press
A Division of Hay House
1663 Liberty Drive
Bloomington, IN 47403
www.balboapress.com
844-682-1282

Because of the dynamic nature of the Internet, any web addresses or links contained in this book may have changed since publication and may no longer be valid. The views expressed in this work are solely those of the author and do not necessarily reflect the views of the publisher, and the publisher hereby disclaims any responsibility for them.

The author of this book does not dispense medical advice or prescribe the use of any technique as a form of treatment for physical, emotional, or medical problems without the advice of a physician, either directly or indirectly. The intent of the author is only to offer information of a general nature to help you in your quest for emotional and spiritual well-being. In the event you use any of the information in this book for yourself, which is your constitutional right, the author and the publisher assume no responsibility for your actions.

Any people depicted in stock imagery provided by Getty Images are models, and such images are being used for illustrative purposes only.
Certain stock imagery © Getty Images.

Print information available on the last page.

ISBN: 979-8-7652-4457-9 (sc)
ISBN: 979-8-7652-4456-2 (e)

Library of Congress Control Number: 2023915215

Balboa Press rev. date: 09/05/2023

Contents

Preface ix

"Echoes of Deception" xi

About the Author xiii

Chapter 1. The Journey Begins 1

Chapter 2. The Complexities of Narcissism 8
Narcissism Defined
Misconceptions About Narcissism
Narcissistic Fuel
Narcissistic Abuse
What is Narcissistic Injury?
A Narcissist in Flight

Chapter 3. Identifying Red Flags 34

Chapter 4. Different flavours of Narcissism 44
Characteristics of a Malignant Narcissist
The Overt vs the Covert Narcissist
The Overt Narcissist
Covert Narcissist
The Narcissistic Parent
The Political Narcissist
The Narcissistic Employer
The Narcissistic Friend
Narcissism and Religious Leaders
The Narcissist in the Military

Chapter 5.   The Retaliation of the Afflicted 69
Narcissism's Role in Criminal Minds
Narcissists are Master Manipulators

**Chapter 6.   Narcissism Co-existing With Other Personality
Disorders** 87
The Psychopath
The Sociopath

**Chapter 7.   Identify Narcissistic Traits in the following
Stories** 97
Rachel's story
Sharmila's Flight

Chapter 8.   The Repercussions of Narcissistic Abuse 103
What type of Individuals do Narcissists target?
The Empath
An Empath's Story
The Super Empath
What Determines a Narcissist or an Empath
growing up under the same Conditions?

Chapter 9.   My story 121
Cycles One to Five
Cycle six – The Pandemic
Cycle seven – My Birthday
Cycle Eight – The mask falls off

Chapter 10. Summary of My Story 178
Flying Monkeys and Enablers
Why do Narcissists get Married?

Chapter 11. Healing from Narcissistic Abuse 187
Self-care after Narcissistic Abuse
Coping mechanisms

Unhealthy Coping Mechanisms
Healthy Coping Mechanisms

Chapter 12. Finding Love After Narcissistic Abuse........... 195
The Aging Narcissist
Have you ever asked yourself, "Am I a narcissist"?
Hope for the Afflicted

An Important Message to Readers.......................................203
Message to the Youths..205
A note to TTNAWH members 207
Conclusion.. 213

Preface

Narcissism has recently become a household topic. It seems as though everyone knows someone who can be called a narcissist. But do they really understand what narcissism is?

Discover the truth behind the mask in "Narcissism Has No Face." Unveiling the captivating depths of narcissistic behavior, this book takes you on a journey of understanding, healing, and empowerment.

Dive into the intricacies of human psychology as you navigate the complexities of narcissism, unravelling its impact on relationships, self-worth, and personal growth. With profound insights and practical guidance, "Narcissism Has No Face" offers a beacon of hope for those seeking to break free from the chains of ignorance and narcissistic influence. Step into a world of self-discovery and reclaim your authentic self.

With engaging illustrative stories, expert analysis, and practical wisdom, you'll learn to navigate narcissistic relationships, recognize the signs, and set healthy boundaries. Empower yourself with knowledge, healing, and personal growth.

Please note that research in this area is on a continuum and therefore the understanding of its complexities is increasing all the time. The information presented in "Narcissism Has No Face" should be used as a guide to understanding the intricacies of personality disorders and their impact on our daily lives.

Never forget that the true catalyst for change resides within you. Your mind is potent, a tool that can shape your reality. The way you use the information you gather is entirely within your control.

Education opens doors, but it's your interpretation and action that pave the way. You hold the brush, crafting the masterpiece of your life. Each decision and response you make contributes to your growth and transformation.

Remember, "Narcissism Has No Face" is to be used as a tutorial, not a diagnostic manual. It is recommended to always seek professional guidance for support and diagnosis.

"Echoes of Deception"

In the depths of trust, I found my heart abused,
By a lover once cherished, but now so confused.
Questions fill my mind, seeking answers that seem far,
How did I miss the signs, the narcissist's dark memoir?

I gave my love freely, with vulnerability untold,
Only to be manipulated, my spirit left cold.
Why wasn't I enough? What did I do wrong?
In this web of deceit, where did I truly belong?

Trusting eyes blinded, by false promises so sweet,
But behind the façade, the narcissist's deceit.
How could love turn to pain, trust into doubt?
I'm left with questions, my heart crying out.

But in the depths of despair, a strength starts to grow,
A glimmer of resilience, a spirit that won't bow.
I'll find the answers, reclaim my shattered heart,
No longer defined by the narcissist's art.

To those who've been hurt, by love's twisted game,
You're not alone in your quest to reclaim your name.
Together we stand, in healing and might,
As we rise above the pain, embracing our light.

About the Author

I am Susan Sylvester-Barker, affectionately called Sue Barker by my clients, colleagues, and followers. At the age of 60, I have an unwavering passion for life and immeasurable gratitude for my journey thus far. I grew up in a middle-class neighbourhood in the tropical islands of Trinidad and Tobago. My educational journey began at Mucurapo Girl's Roman Catholic School, laying the foundation for my academic pursuits.

After completing my primary schooling, I attended two consecutive secondary schools to continue my education. Subsequently, I pursued studies in various tertiary and career-oriented organizations, earning certificates and awards in the fields of marketing and finance.

Throughout my adult life, I have been fortunate to have opportunities that allowed me to work and further, my education, providing invaluable experiences and fostering personal and professional growth.

For the past twenty-six years, I have had the privilege of being a part of the finance industry. Currently, I serve as an Insurance Advisor with an American-based insurance company operating in Trinidad and Tobago. Additionally, I am the President and Founder of the Trinidad and Tobago Narcissistic Awareness and Healing (TTNAWH) Foundation, an NGO that raises awareness and provides support for victims of narcissistic abuse.

Five years ago, at the age of fifty-five, I found myself entangled in a perplexing situation with an individual exhibiting the traits of a narcissist. It was an emotionally draining experience that left me feeling betrayed and embarrassed. However, through extensive research, self-awareness, and education on narcissism, I was able to rise above the entanglement, empowered and equipped to share my findings with others who may be on a similar journey.

Education and awareness about narcissism are critical on this journey because this is what guarantees liberation from this type of abuse. My thirst for knowledge and the ability to share it with the least suspecting continues up to this day. I have become an avid psychology enthusiast and am currently pursuing a degree in the subject at Saylor Academy. Exploring the intricate workings of the human brain's neurological processes has intrigued me. I am also pursuing further studies in finance at The American College, ensuring that I stay well-versed in the ever-evolving financial landscape.

I am grateful for the support of my three children, their families and friends, a small group of my friends, and members of the TTNAWH Foundation.

Despite the challenges I faced, I dedicated more time and effort to earn several industry awards, which granted me the opportunity to travel to countries inclusive of Germany, England, Jamaica, and Barbados, with all expenses covered by the company. I consider myself truly blessed to be a part of this organization.

I now share my first book in the series, "Narcissism Has No Face," with you, hoping that its contents serve as a tool to assist you in understanding the dynamics of narcissism. The objective is that you would gain a better understanding of how this complex and multifaceted personality disorder affects our lives daily.

"The first step towards change is awareness."
- Nathaniel Branden

Chapter One
The Journey Begins

The TTNAWH, (Trinidad and Tobago Narcissistic Awareness and Healing for Women) was created as a support group for women. The group was formed while on my journey for answers to the questions in the foregoing poem "Echoes of Deception". The beginning of that journey pointed me in the direction of Personality Disorders.

I started my research on bipolar disorder but that was not providing the answers to the questions I had, regarding my relationship with an individual I will call Damien. After some time researching and comparing the characteristics of this individual, I was convinced that Narcissism was the culprit behind what I had experienced with Damien. It was unbelievable how accurately this newfound knowledge described my situation.

Subsequently, I spent over four years researching narcissism or narcissistic personality disorder, (NPD), the clinical name for this condition. Narcissism was first identified as a mental disorder by the British essayist Havelock Ellis in 1898. However, NPD was officially recognized in the third edition of the Diagnostic and Statistical Manual of Mental Disorders (DSM-3) in 1980. The current criteria for NPD were established in the fifth edition of (DSM-5) in 2013.

The information I was being privy to suggested that Narcissism would have played a great role in certain experiences that led me to this point in my life that was unexplainable. I needed to find a support system, other than my family and friends, that was knowledgeable enough to answer my questions. I searched online and made some calls to different organizations locally, but soon realized, there were no support groups available locally to assist with the understanding of what Narcissism is and the way this complex mechanism affects our daily lives.

I had certainly heard the term before but had no reason to pay attention to what it meant until now. Now that the word "Narcissist" is popping up everywhere my awareness has certainly gone into overdrive. The research along with my experiences made me wonder, "How many persons today understand what Narcissism is?" The word is used loosely to describe someone who has a grandiose personality, is arrogant, has a sense of entitlement, and lacks empathy, to say the least.

I was in that category of ignorance a few years ago like so many others. That was until I had the experience of being in a romantic relationship as mentioned, with someone displaying these traits. In fairness to him, he was not aware that his behavior was actually on a spectrum and that it could be diagnosed. He just behaved the only way he knew how and found nothing bad about it at the time. But we'll get into that later on.

The severity of mental, psychological, and emotional abuse, that persons who are ensnared by someone afflicted with Narcissism is on a level I never knew existed in all my years. This led to many questions that I could not get answers to until I began my quest. This journey led me to find answers not only to the questions I had but answers to questions a whole lot of other people are struggling to answer even now. I am realizing daily that because of the number of people who are suffering abuse from someone with Narcissism, it can or should be categorized as a Global Pandemic.

To understand more about Narcissism and to get some support on my journey to healing, I joined an international Narcissistic Awareness Community, where I connected with several women who were either victims or survivors of Narcissistic Abuse. They were sharing their stories in the hope of getting support and relief just as I was hoping to. It was definitely the place to be!

This was when it hit me, "I need to speak to women in our local communities about what I was discovering!" Those that are suffering in situations of domestic violence that are crying out daily, but more so for the ones that don't cry out but stay and suffer in silence. I especially needed them to hear a voice of hope.

I had to find a way to make a difference, to help them understand that "they are enough," and that they were not to blame for their circumstances. When I examined the demographics of this International Community of women who are experiencing this sort of abuse, and crying out for help, it was so overwhelming. They are people from various countries around the world, with diverse backgrounds, different ethnicity, age groups, and professions, stemming from all walks of life.

When I joined that group there were just over four thousand members. Five years later we are now over fifty thousand and counting. We have sub-communities inside the initial community, all seeking to save their sanity and find a better way of living. I am now a firm believer in the fact that we underrate "peace of mind". It's priceless!

I then asked myself, "What makes us different on this twin island?" I was convinced that locally, we needed that kind of support too. Our women are suffering just as much and needed a safe place where they can get the education, support, and healing necessary for them to rescue themselves from this horrific type of abuse. A type of abuse unless it is physical is not recognized. And trust me it gets there also.

Since the birth of TTNAWH in 2018, I have had the privilege of interacting with several women throughout our local communities. These women all have one thing in common. They were all looking for answers just as I was. Many have joined the TTNAWH foundation and are on their way to finding the answers that would make a positive difference in their lives.

They are given support as well as guidance on how to research for answers because although some characteristics are similar, there can be varying differences also. Everyone's experience is unique, but all the information is out there! You just have to know where to look and what to look for.

We support each other on this journey as we are gaining more knowledge to overcome the ill effects of this disorder every day. We are united on this journey because Narcissism is not my issue or your issue, it is a societal issue.

I have been interviewed by Television and Radio hosts regarding my journey and the feedback is always the same. People are always in awe at what they hear and want to know more about this complex mechanism that is Narcissism. I remember one time when the Radio show was finished, I had forty-seven missed calls on my cell phone from persons who tried to call while the program was still in process. The minute I gave out my number on the show, the calls began pouring in.

The responses I receive on this journey are nothing short of humbling. People are looking for answers to the same questions I had, and this motivates me to continue on this journey. My mission is to continue to share my knowledge, experiences and stories so others can be made aware of the effects of this underlying mental condition. The information is literally lifesaving!

I consider it a great privilege to be able to share the knowledge and experience I have acquired on this journey. I have developed a passion for what I do because many individuals have benefitted from the awareness I raise, and they continue to support this initiative. Life/experience is indeed the greatest teacher.

With the exposure that I received in the media, men began reaching out to me for answers as well. In light of that, I began accepting their requests to join the group and changed the name from Trinidad and Tobago Narcissistic Awareness and Healing for Women to just Trinidad and Tobago Narcissistic Awareness and Healing (TTNAWH) Foundation.

We are now an NGO and although our mission is to raise awareness, we also try to support members in the community that may need more than just a listening ear. You will be surprised at the number of Narcissistic women that exists in our Society!

I was shocked to learn that women suffer from this mental condition as well as men since men are always seen as the perpetrator in abusive relationships. Subsequently, I decided to include "the effects Narcissism have on the male" in my research and study routine.

When I heard stories from these men who suffered at the hands of Narcissistic women, it was a real eye-opener. I think their experiences are worst in some way since men are more egotistical and looked upon as the stronger sex or the aggressor in the relationship. The world can be cruel at times, so sometimes when men open up about their situations they are laughed at and accused of being weak. Whereas, when women speak out, they usually attract empathy/sympathy.

The Cleveland Clinic published an article in June 2020, stating that at least 5% of the world's population suffers from Narcissistic Personality Disorder (NPD). Also, in 2018 a team of Medical Professionals from the American Psychology Association noted in an article published on Google, that "20% of the military population has Narcissistic traits". It is also said from other research that one in four persons, suffers from other types of Personality Disorders that can also co-exist with Narcissism. Just keep that in mind as you continue reading.

"Through self-awareness and strength,
I can free myself from the chains of
narcissism and reclaim my power."
Sue Barker

Chapter Two
The Complexities of Narcissism
Narcissism Defined

Due to the complexities of neurological processes, it would be helpful if you make note of the following intricacies of personality characteristics and traits, as you explore the diverse spectrum of personality disorders. It is important to note that certain traits may be present in multiple personality types or may overlap to some extent.

This is because the foundation of humanism in the neurological process allows for shared foundational traits, while the severity and manifestation of personality disorders can introduce variations.

As you delve deeper into your understanding, I encourage you to pay close attention to the nuances and subtleties that distinguish each trait, even if they may initially appear similar in nature. These differences contribute to the unique flavours and expressions of each personality type, providing valuable insights into the complexities of human behavior and psychology.

Remember that individuals are multifaceted, and their personalities can manifest in a range of ways. Embracing the diversity and intricacy of human nature allows for a richer and more comprehensive understanding of the multifaceted tapestry of personalities. This can be attributed to the fact that narcissism exists on a spectrum, and individuals may exhibit varying degrees of narcissistic traits. Not all traits associated with narcissism may be present in every individual, and the intensity of these traits can differ

Narcissistic traits can range from an excessive need for admiration and a grandiose sense of self-importance to a lack of empathy and an exploitative approach in relationships. However, the prominence and combination of these traits can vary among individuals. Some individuals may display more pronounced characteristics of grandiosity and a relentless pursuit of attention and admiration, while others may exhibit more subtle signs of narcissism that are less apparent in their everyday interactions.

It is important to recognize that the presence of certain narcissistic traits does not necessarily indicate a full-blown Narcissistic Personality Disorder (NPD). NPD is diagnosed when these traits significantly impair an individual's functioning and cause distress.

During the formative years, the brain undergoes significant development, and the way data is received and processed by different parts of the brain is crucial to this process. Neurological mechanisms such as neurotransmission, trafficking, cellular homeostasis, and inflammation all contribute to the development of the individual's personality. The characteristics and experiences embedded during this period can have long-lasting effects, whether positive or negative.

To put it simply, the central nervous system consists of two main bodies of tissues, grey matter and white matter. Grey matter refers to the regions of the brain that primarily consist of neuronal cell bodies, dendrites, and synapses. It is involved in various cognitive processes, including perception, decision-making, and emotion regulation. Within the grey matter, specific brain regions such as the prefrontal cortex, amygdala, and anterior cingulate cortex are particularly relevant in this regard.

Grey matter contains a large number of neurons that process information and communicate new information through axon signalling, which is facilitated by the white matter. It is also involved in controlling movement, memory, and emotions, and it plays a significant role in various aspects of human life.

Both grey matter and white matter are vital for the transmission of signals, to and from the brain and spinal cord, allowing us to function normally. Understanding the importance of these brain structures helps us appreciate the intricate relationship between brain development, emotions, and overall functioning.

In the context of coping mechanisms and emotional regulation, both grey matter and white matter in the brain play important roles. The prefrontal cortex, located in the frontal lobe, is responsible for higher-order cognitive functions, including self-control, decision-making, and planning. It plays a critical role in regulating emotions and employing adaptive coping strategies.

The prefrontal cortex helps individuals evaluate the potential consequences of their actions, modulate emotional responses, and make informed choices about which coping mechanisms to utilize in a given situation.

The amygdala, a structure deep within the brain's temporal lobe, is involved in the processing and regulation of emotions, particularly fear and anxiety. It plays a crucial role in the initial detection of emotional stimuli and the generation of emotional responses. Dysfunction in the amygdala can contribute to difficulties in emotional regulation and the selection of appropriate coping strategies.

White matter, on the other hand, refers to the parts of the brain composed of nerve fibres called axons that form connections between different regions of grey matter. These connections enable communication and information exchange across different brain regions. White matter is primarily responsible for transmitting electrical signals and facilitating the coordination of neural networks.

White matter pathways, such as the corpus callosum and various association fibers, are essential for integrating information from different brain regions involved in emotion regulation and coping. These pathways facilitate communication between the prefrontal cortex, amygdala, and other structures also involved in emotional processing, allowing for coordinated responses and the implementation of adaptive coping strategies.

In summary, grey matter regions such as the prefrontal cortex and amygdala are critical for emotional regulation and decision-making, while white matter pathways enable the integration and communication between these brain regions. Both grey matter and white matter contribute significantly to the complex processes involved in coping mechanisms and emotional regulation, ensuring effective responses to stress and emotional challenges.

Coping mechanisms are strategies or behaviors that people use to manage stress, regulate emotions, and find relief. They can be conscious or unconscious, and their effectiveness can vary depending on the situation and individual. Here are some coping mechanisms and their effects often deployed by individuals:

- **Distancing:** Distancing oneself from a situation, whether physically or emotionally, can be a coping mechanism to find peace or prevent escalating tension. It can be a positive strategy as long as it doesn't lead to prolonged isolation or avoidance of necessary interactions.

- **No Contact:** No contact refers to completely cutting off communication and interactions with a toxic person or situation. It can be a severe form of distancing, employed to protect oneself from further harm or toxicity.

- **Crying:** Crying can serve as a coping mechanism to express and release emotions. It can provide relief and catharsis in both positive and negative situations, such as sadness, disappointment, joy, or overwhelming emotions.

- **Talking/Psychotherapy**: Engaging in conversation, whether with a trusted person or a professional therapist, can be a positive coping mechanism. It allows individuals to share their thoughts, emotions, and problems, gaining insight, support, and relief in the process.

- **Self-Harming:** Self-harming, such as cutting or self-inflicted injuries, is a negative coping mechanism. It is an unhealthy way of dealing with emotional pain and trauma. It can serve as a temporary distraction from underlying pain but does not address the root causes and can lead to further harm.

- **Addictions:** Substance abuse, such as drugs or alcohol, and behavioral addictions like gambling or sex addiction, can serve as coping mechanisms to temporarily escape or numb emotional pain. These addictive behaviors stimulate the release of dopamine, (one of the happy hormones), providing a temporary sense of pleasure or relief. However, over time, addictions can have severe negative consequences for individuals and their relationships, leading to physical, psychological, and social harm.

- **Narcissism** is also a coping mechanism, particularly in the context of narcissistic personality disorder (NPD). It's a very powerful and complex mechanism but, hugely effective in helping the afflicted one cope with the world around them. Individuals with NPD develop narcissistic traits as a way to cope with deep-seated insecurities and, a lack of control over their environment.

It is also used as a protective or defence mechanism by the afflicted one as needed, to maintain a sense of self-worth and control. While narcissism may provide relief for the afflicted individual, it often causes significant harm to their relationships and interactions with others.

The development of narcissism is believed to be influenced by two constructs, a genetic predisposition and the lack of control environment. Genetic predispositions may contribute to certain personality traits, while the environment, including childhood experiences and upbringing, plays a pivotal role in shaping and reinforcing narcissistic tendencies.

It is indeed true that certain characteristics, both physical and behavioral, can be inherited from our ancestors through our genes. These factors work together, like the seed and soil analogy, to form the basis of narcissistic traits. The genetic predisposition being the seed and the lack of controlled environment being the soil.

When exploring the origins of Narcissistic Personality Disorder (NPD) or narcissistic tendencies, it can be informative to investigate the individual's upbringing and familial background. Research suggests that there can be a correlation between parental narcissism or the presence of other personality disorders within the family and, the development of narcissistic traits in a child.

This information can be valuable when considering long-term commitments or relationships with someone displaying narcissistic tendencies.

Growing up in an ideal home with two loving parents who provide their child/children with food, shelter, clothing, and a loving and peaceful environment is golden. But, unfortunately, not every child has that luxury.

It is heart-wrenching, to say the least when you hear or witness some of the traumatic events that some children are exposed to in their early development. Needless to say, child abuse is on the rise evidenced by reports on various websites including cdc.gov, which stated that "At least 1 in 7 children have experienced child abuse or neglect in the past year", and that's just in the United States alone.

"Child maltreatment, particularly neglect and emotional abuse, can cause long-term, critical impairment to brain functions" (childwelfare.gov reports) it continues, "These alterations can affect memory, self-control and responses to stress." It is no wonder why we see unpleasant behaviors being manifested in children at schools. In addition, there are widespread reports of sexual abuse, abandonment, physical abuse, omission, and pressure to always live up to their caregiver's expectations.

Another scenario is when the child is over-compensated for small achievements or considered the golden child. A host of mental conditions can arise as a result of exposure to the foregoing stressors, including but not limited to:

- **Post-Traumatic Stress Disorder (PTSD)**: PTSD is a mental health condition that can develop in individuals who have experienced or witnessed a traumatic event. Symptoms include intrusive thoughts or memories, nightmares, flashbacks, hypervigilance, avoidance of reminders of the trauma, and changes in mood and cognition.

- **Depression:** Depression is a mood disorder characterized by persistent feelings of sadness, loss of interest or pleasure in activities, changes in appetite or weight, sleep disturbances, low energy, difficulty concentrating, feelings of guilt or worthlessness, and thoughts of self-harm or suicide.

- **Acute Stress Disorder:** Acute stress disorder occurs in response to a traumatic event and involves symptoms similar to PTSD, such as intrusive thoughts, avoidance behaviors, negative mood, dissociation, and heightened arousal. However, the symptoms are experienced for a shorter duration, typically within the first month following the trauma.

- **Adjustment Disorders:** Adjustment disorders occur when an individual has difficulty coping with and adjusting to stressful life events. Symptoms may include emotional distress, behavioral changes, impaired social or occupational functioning, and a sense of being overwhelmed.

- **Reactive Attachment Disorder (RAD):** RAD typically develops in children who have experienced severe neglect, abuse, or disruptions in early caregiving relationships. It is characterized by difficulties in forming and maintaining healthy attachments, social withdrawal, emotional dysregulation, and problems with trust and intimacy.

- **Disinhibited Social Engagement Disorder (DSED):** DSED is also seen in children who have experienced early neglect or disruptions in caregiving. It involves a lack of appropriate fear or wariness of strangers, overly familiar or indiscriminate behavior with unfamiliar individuals, and impaired social boundaries.

- **Unclassified and Unspecified Trauma Disorder:** These terms are used to describe trauma-related conditions that do not fit specific diagnostic criteria for other disorders. They may involve various symptoms related to trauma, such as anxiety, mood disturbances, or difficulties in functioning, but do not meet the full criteria for a specific disorder.

- **Shame:** Shame is a powerful feeling of embarrassment, guilt, or humiliation that arises from a belief or perception of having done something wrong, immoral, or socially unacceptable. It often involves a negative evaluation of oneself and can result in feelings of inadequacy, self-consciousness, and a desire to hide or withdraw from others.

- **Fear:** Fear is an emotional response to a perceived threat or danger. It is a natural and instinctive reaction that prepares the body for a "fight or flight" response. Fear can range from mild unease to intense terror and can be triggered by real or imagined situations.

- **Lack of control:** Lack of control refers to a situation or feeling where an individual perceives a loss or absence of power or influence over their own actions, decisions, or circumstances. It can lead to feelings of helplessness, frustration, and anxiety.

- **Neglect:** Neglect is the failure to provide proper care, attention, or support to someone who is dependent on it. It can occur in various forms, such as physical, emotional, or educational neglect. Neglect can have detrimental effects on a person's well-being and development.

- **Shifting sands:** "Shifting sands" is a metaphorical expression used to describe a situation or circumstance that is constantly changing or unstable, making it difficult to establish a firm foundation or make reliable predictions. It refers to an environment or situation where circumstances, opinions, or conditions are subject to frequent and unpredictable shifts.

The term "shifting sands" is often used to convey the idea that one cannot rely on a stable or fixed state of affairs. It suggests that any plans, decisions, or expectations made within this context may be rendered irrelevant or ineffective due to the ever-changing nature of the circumstances.

In a broader sense, "shifting sands" can also symbolize uncertainty, unpredictability, or a lack of stability in various aspects of life, such as relationships, careers, or societal dynamics. It serves as a reminder to be adaptable, flexible, and responsive to change, as well as to approach situations with caution and a willingness to adjust plans as needed.

The phrase is derived from the literal shifting of dunes in deserts or along coastlines due to wind, water, or other natural forces. The landscape of sand constantly changes, making it difficult to establish fixed paths or structures. The metaphorical use of "shifting sands" captures this concept of constant change and instability in different contexts.

- **The golden child syndrome:** The golden child syndrome is a term commonly used in the context of dysfunctional family dynamics, particularly in narcissistic or abusive families. It describes a situation where one child is favoured and idealized by the parent or caregiver, often at the expense of other siblings.

The golden child is often perceived as "perfect" or "special" and receives preferential treatment, while other siblings may experience neglect or abuse.

- **Isolation:** Isolation refers to a state of being separated, detached, or cut off from others. It can be physical, where a person is physically removed from social contact, or emotional, where an individual feels disconnected or alienated from others. Isolation can lead to feelings of loneliness, depression, and a lack of social support.

- **Omission:** Omission refers to the act of leaving something out or failing to include or mention it. It can involve intentionally or unintentionally excluding or neglecting important information, details, or actions. Omission can have significant consequences, as it may distort or misrepresent a situation or communication.

- **Physical pain:** Physical pain refers to the unpleasant sensory and emotional experience that arises from actual or potential tissue damage. It is typically associated with a physical injury, illness, or disease. Physical pain can range from mild discomfort to severe agony and is an important protective mechanism that alerts the body to potential harm or injury.

In instances when a child is subjected to less-than-ideal living conditions, there can be extreme abuse that causes excessive stress and tumultuous pain. These conditions cause that child's natural development to be interrupted. This is called arrested development.

This arrested development forms a new personality to help the underdeveloped child to cope with the traumatic events that he/she is not in control of at that time. When this happens, the child will now develop characteristics to allow him to survive in that same environment.

However, the new personality will only be interested in providing a coping mechanism for that child, no one else. It imprisons the true self/personality to protect the child from its environment. That's when "NARCISSISM" is formed!

Narcissism will protect the underdeveloped personality from the conscious state of shame, fear, lack of control, neglect, shifting sands, the golden child syndrome, isolation, omission, and even physical pain.

Remember I mentioned the "grey matter" and the "white matter" and the importance of these bodies of tissue in the transportation of the essential neurons, nerve cells, and all the other intricate parts of the central nervous system? Remember how crucial the role of each is in achieving the systematic functions of typical human living?

If you have any questions about this, go back and read the paragraph on it before you proceed.

Get this! An article from Yale.news.edu dated 9th January, 2012 stated the following, "Experiencing stressful life events can reduce grey matter in critical regions of the brain that regulate emotion and important physiological functions".

In an experiment done by the American Psychology Association using magnetic resonance imaging (MRI) to scan the brain of patients diagnosed with NPD vs healthy persons, it was discovered that "pathological Narcissists" have less grey matter in the left anterior insular than healthy persons do."

The study is ongoing, and the full report is available online. Also, in another article from sciencedaily.com dated 24/2/2012, it states that "an international team led by researchers at Mount Sinai School of Medicine in New York has for the first time shown that one area of the brain, called the anterior insular cortex, is the activity centre of human empathy, whereas other areas of the brain are not."

It's worth noting that research in this field is ongoing, and the relationship between brain structure, functioning, and specific personality disorders like NPD is complex and multifaceted. While studies have identified certain brain regions and their involvement in empathy, emotion regulation, and self-related processing, the exact mechanisms and causality between brain changes and the development of Narcissistic traits are still being explored.

Misconceptions About Narcissism

Misconceptions about narcissism are common and can lead to misunderstandings about the condition and its impact on individuals and relationships. Here are some prevalent misconceptions:

Narcissism is just excessive self-love: While narcissists may have an inflated sense of self-importance, narcissism goes beyond healthy self-confidence. It involves a pattern of grandiosity, a lack of empathy, and exploiting others for personal gain.

All narcissists are the same: Narcissism exists on a spectrum, and not all individuals with narcissistic traits or narcissistic personality disorder (NPD) will display the same behaviors. Some may be more overt and abrasive, while others may be covert and manipulative.

Narcissists are always confident: While they may portray a confident facade, many narcissists have fragile self-esteem and use their grandiosity to mask feelings of inadequacy or insecurity.

Narcissism is untreatable: While personality disorders like NPD can be challenging to treat, there are therapeutic approaches that can help individuals with narcissistic traits develop healthier behaviors and coping mechanisms. The challenge remains in getting them to agree and respond to therapy when narcissism protects them from seeing their shortcomings.

Narcissism is just a result of bad parenting: While early life experiences can influence personality development, narcissism is a complex condition that has genetic, environmental, and social factors contributing to its manifestation.

Narcissists can't have successful relationships: Narcissists can be charming and charismatic, making it possible to attract and maintain relationships, at least initially. However, their exploitative and self-centred tendencies often lead to difficulties in sustaining healthy, long-term connections.

Narcissism is always obvious: Some narcissists may be overt and attention-seeking, but others may present as charming, compassionate, and even victimized, making it harder to identify their manipulative behaviors.

Only men can be narcissists: Narcissism can affect people of any gender. While research has shown a higher prevalence of NPD in men, women can also exhibit narcissistic traits or have NPD.

Narcissism is a choice: Narcissistic traits and disorders are complex and likely result from a combination of psychological, genetic, and environmental factors. While individuals can learn to manage their behaviors, the root causes may not always be consciously chosen.

Narcissism is always abusive: While narcissistic behaviors can be emotionally damaging, not all narcissists are physically or emotionally abusive. Some may display manipulative and exploitative tendencies without resorting to physical violence.

Understanding the true nature of narcissism is essential for recognizing and addressing it appropriately in personal and professional relationships. It's crucial to approach the subject with compassion and awareness of the complexities involved.

Narcissistic Fuel

A narcissist needs three key elements to thrive. Control, specific character traits, and residual benefits. These components form the foundation for their existence and enable their manipulative tendencies. These three components can be gained from various sources in their matrix and are termed narcissistic fuel.

Emotional responses, whether good or bad provides the most potent fuel for the narcissist and usually come from a primary source. Whether the responses are indicative of pleasure, fury, or pain, it doesn't matter, the prime aim is to assert control of the victim. come

Lastly, narcissists derive residual benefits from their relationships, exploiting others for personal gain and self-gratification. Together, these elements sustain the narcissist's survival in their pursuit of fulfilling their own needs at the expense of those around them. Once this is achieved it satisfies the narcissist's objective and they can now feel comfortable to move on to their next level of manipulation. Here are some of the characteristics that feed the narcissist's insatiable ego:

- **Control and power:** Narcissists have an intense need for control and power over others. They often manipulate and exploit people to assert their dominance and maintain a sense of superiority. Controlling others' thoughts, emotions, and actions provides a sense of security and validation for them. Narcissists prioritize their own needs, desires, and interests above others. They require an environment where their desires are prioritized and catered to, without considering the needs or feelings of those around them.

- **Admiration and adoration:** Narcissists crave constant admiration and adoration from others. They need to be seen as special, exceptional, and superior. Without external validation and admiration, their self-esteem can plummet, leading to feelings of insecurity and vulnerability.

- **Manipulation and exploitation:** Narcissists often engage in manipulative tactics and exploit others for their gain. They may use charm, deceit, or coercion to achieve their objectives and fulfil their needs, without regard for the well-being or feelings of others.

- **Self-idealization:** Narcissists have a grandiose self-image and require continuous reinforcement of their idealized version of themselves. They need to be seen as perfect, superior, and faultless. Any perceived criticism or challenge to their idealized self can be met with defensiveness or hostility.

- **Lack of accountability:** Narcissists often evade taking responsibility for their actions and deflect blame onto others. They struggle with admitting faults or accepting consequences for their behavior, as it threatens their self-image of being flawless and superior.

- **Triangulation:** Triangulation is a manipulation tactic commonly used by individuals, including narcissists, to manipulate or control relationships and situations. It involves bringing a third party into a conflict or relationship dynamic to shift the power balance or gain an advantage. In the context of interpersonal relationships, triangulation typically plays out as follows:

- **The manipulator:** The individual initiating the triangulation is usually the one seeking to manipulate or control the situation. This person may be a narcissist, but not necessarily. They may be motivated by a desire for attention, validation, or power over others.

- **The target:** The target is the person who becomes entangled in the triangulation. This individual is often the primary focus of the manipulator's tactics and maybe a partner, family member, friend, or colleague.

- **The third party:** The manipulator brings in a third person, often an ally or confidant, to support their position or undermine the target. This third party is usually unaware of the manipulator's true intentions and may unknowingly become a pawn in the manipulation.

The purpose of triangulation can vary, but common objectives are as follows:

- **Creating confusion and doubt:** By involving a third party, the manipulator seeks to confuse the target and undermine their confidence in their own perceptions or judgments. This can make the target more dependent on the manipulator for guidance or validation.

- **Controlling information flow:** Triangulation allows the manipulator to control the narrative by selectively sharing information or distorting the truth. They may use a third party to spread rumours, provide misinformation, or create a distorted version of events that supports their agenda.

- **Provoking jealousy or competition:** Triangulation can be used to evoke feelings of jealousy or competition in the target. By involving a third person who may appear more favourable or desirable, the manipulator aims to create tension and insecurity within the relationship.

- **Strengthening their position**: The manipulator may use triangulation to bolster their sense of power or superiority. By aligning themselves with a third party, they may feel more confident in asserting their authority or control over the target.

- **Gender differences:** Some studies suggest that narcissistic traits may be more prevalent in males than females. However, it's important to differentiate between clinical Narcissistic Personality Disorders (NPD) and narcissistic traits in the general population. While research indicates a higher prevalence of NPD in males, there is debate around whether there are true gender differences or if it is influenced by societal factors and diagnostic bias.

- **Narcissistic Personality Disorder (NPD):** Studies estimate that around 0.5-1% of the general population meets the criteria for NPD. However, these estimates can vary depending on the specific sample and diagnostic criteria used. NPD is more commonly diagnosed in males than females, but it's essential to recognize that narcissistic traits can exist across genders.

Narcissistic traits in the general population: Research suggests that narcissistic traits, which may not meet the diagnostic threshold for NPD, are relatively common in both men and women. Studies have found that men tend to score slightly higher on measures of grandiose narcissism, characterized by assertiveness and a desire for dominance, while women may score slightly higher on measures of vulnerable narcissism, characterized by insecurity, low self-esteem, and emotional distress.

Please be reminded that it is important to approach these statistics with caution, as narcissism is a complex and multifaceted construct that can manifest differently in individuals. Additionally, cultural and contextual factors can influence the expression and assessment of narcissistic traits.

While these elements are perceived as necessary for a narcissist's survival, they can also contribute to their dysfunctional behaviors and the negative impact they have on their relationships and others around them.

There is absolutely no doubt in my mind that dealing with a narcissistic individual can be emotionally challenging and potentially harmful in every way. It is advisable to prioritize your well-being and safety. If you find yourself in a situation where the narcissistic behavior is causing significant distress or harm, seeking professional guidance from therapists or counsellors who specialize in narcissistic abuse can be beneficial.

They can provide guidance, support, and strategies for coping with the challenges posed by narcissistic individuals.

However, if several attempts at seeking outside intervention do not help, it is advisable that you use discernment in assessing your experiences with any individual possessing these traits. Surrounding yourself with a strong support system and practicing self-compassion can help you navigate the complexities of such relationships.

Whatever options you choose, you should ensure you practice self-care, setting healthy boundaries and joining a support group. Do not suffer in silence by isolating yourself!

Narcissistic Abuse

Narcissistic abuse refers to the pattern of harmful and manipulative behavior exhibited by individuals with narcissistic personality disorder (NPD) or narcissistic traits. It involves the systematic and intentional exploitation, manipulation, and control of another person for the narcissist's own gratification and self-centred needs.

Narcissistic abuse can occur in various types of relationships, including romantic partnerships, family relationships, friendships, or even within professional settings. The abuse is characterized by a range of tactics aimed at undermining the victim's self-esteem, autonomy, and well-being. Some common forms of narcissistic abuse include:

- **Emotional manipulation:** Narcissists use tactics such as gaslighting, where they distort reality, manipulate the victim's perception, and make them doubt their memory, emotions, and sanity. They may also employ guilt-tripping, blaming, or shaming techniques to control and manipulate the victim's emotions.

- **Verbal and psychological abuse:** Narcissists engage in constant criticism, insults, put-downs, and belittling of their victims. They may engage in name-calling, demeaning remarks, and personal attacks to maintain power and control over the victim.

- **Exploitation and disregard for boundaries:** Narcissists view others as objects to fulfil their needs and desires. They exploit and manipulate the victim's vulnerabilities, emotions, and resources for their own gain. They may disregard the victim's boundaries, invade their privacy, or use their personal information against them.

- **Isolation and control:** Narcissists often isolate their victims from friends, family, and support systems to maintain control and dependency. They may manipulate the victim's social interactions, restrict their activities, or undermine their independence to keep them under their influence.

- **Intermittent reinforcement:** Narcissists employ a cycle of idealization and devaluation. They initially shower the victim with excessive attention, affection, and admiration (love bombing), making the victim feel special and valued. However, they then devalue and discard the victim, subjecting them to emotional neglect, indifference, or even hostility, which creates a cycle of confusion and emotional dependency.

Narcissistic abuse can have severe and long-lasting effects on the victim's mental, emotional, and physical well-being. It is crucial for victims of narcissistic abuse to seek support, therapy, establish strong boundaries to protect themselves, and begin the process of healing and recovery.

What is Narcissistic Injury?

Narcissistic injury refers to the emotional and psychological harm experienced by narcissistic individuals when their inflated self-image is challenged, criticized, or threatened. It occurs when something or someone confronts the narcissist with evidence that contradicts their grandiose self-perception, exposes their flaws or failures, or challenges their sense of superiority and entitlement.

When a narcissist experiences narcissistic injury, it can trigger a range of defensive reactions and behaviors aimed at preserving their self-esteem and protecting their fragile ego. These reactions may include:

- **Rage and Anger:** Narcissists may respond to narcissistic injury with intense anger or rage. They may become verbally or even physically aggressive, lashing out at those they perceive as the source of the injury.

- **Defensiveness:** Narcissists often have a strong need to defend their self-image and may become excessively defensive when their flaws or mistakes are pointed out. They may deny responsibility, make excuses, or deflect blame onto others.

- **Withdrawal and Silent Treatment:** In some cases, narcissists may retreat and give the silent treatment as a way of avoiding further injury or confrontation. They may cut off communication or emotionally distance themselves from the situation or individuals involved.

- **Invalidating Others:** To protect their self-image, narcissists may invalidate or dismiss the feelings, perspectives, or experiences of others. They may belittle or undermine those who challenge their self-perception, attempting to regain a sense of superiority.

- **Seeking Narcissistic Fuel:** Following a narcissistic injury, some individuals may intensify their efforts to seek external validation and attention (known as narcissistic fuel). They may engage in attention-seeking behaviors or manipulate others to regain a sense of self-worth.

It's important to note that narcissistic injury is an inherent part of the narcissistic personality structure, where individuals have a deep-seated need for admiration, validation, and a fragile self-esteem. Understanding narcissistic injury can provide insights into the behavior of individuals with narcissistic traits, but it is crucial to approach these situations with caution and seek support from professionals who specialize in dealing with narcissistic personality dynamics.

A Narcissist in Flight

The term "Narcissist in flight" typically refers to a situation where a narcissistic individual engages in avoidance or escapism behaviors to protect their self-image and avoid facing criticism, confrontation, or accountability for their actions. It is a defensive response that narcissists employ when they feel threatened or when their fragile self-esteem is at risk of being exposed.

When a narcissist is in flight, they may employ various tactics to avoid responsibility or maintain their inflated self-perception.

These tactics can include:

• **Withdrawal:** The narcissist may physically or emotionally withdraw from a situation or relationship when they perceive it as threatening or when they fear negative feedback.

• **Deflection:** They may redirect blame or criticism onto others, deflecting attention away from them and onto someone or something else. This is often done through manipulation, gaslighting, or shifting the focus of the conversation.

• **Avoidance:** Narcissists may actively avoid situations or interactions that challenge their self-image or expose their flaws. This can involve evading discussions, ignoring messages or requests for accountability, or physically removing themselves from the situation.

- **Projection:** They may project their negative qualities, insecurities, or behaviors onto others, essentially accusing others of the very things they are guilty of. This allows them to avoid self-reflection and maintain their sense of superiority.

- **Disengagement:** Narcissists may disengage or cut off relationships abruptly when they feel their ego is being threatened or when they believe they can no longer control the narrative. This can leave others feeling confused, hurt, or abandoned.

It's important to note that these behaviors are characteristic of individuals with narcissistic personality traits or narcissistic personality disorder. Understanding these patterns of behavior can be helpful for those dealing with narcissistic individuals in their lives, but it's essential to approach such situations with care and seek professional guidance if needed.

"Forewarned is forearmed."
Miguel de Cervantes

Chapter Three
Identifying Red Flags

While these traits can be indicative of narcissism, it is not a definitive diagnosis. Only a qualified mental health professional can diagnose someone with Narcissistic Personality Disorder (NPD). However, the following traits are commonly associated with narcissism and can serve as red flags:

- **Lack of empathy:** A prominent characteristic of a narcissist is their *lack of empathy*. Empathy refers to the ability to understand and share the feelings of others, to put oneself in someone else's shoes, and experience their emotions. Narcissists, as a result of their coping mechanism and arrested development, struggle to empathize with others on an emotional level.

The development of narcissism as a coping mechanism is primarily focused on protecting the underdeveloped self from the pain, shame, and distress associated with their traumatic and lack of control experiences. Narcissists are often preoccupied with their own needs, desires, and self-image, which leave little room for genuine empathy towards others.

This explains why victims of narcissistic abuse often endure significant suffering at the hands of a narcissist. It's important to understand that narcissists are incapable of experiencing empathy, not because they don't want to, it's just because they are wired differently.

As one of my influential teachers explained, "A narcissist will step over an elderly person who has fallen on the roadside, without showing any concern and, go about their business like normal."

This is because their reactions are driven by instinct rather than emotional empathy. In contrast, individuals without narcissism would typically have an emotional response that would motivate them to offer assistance due to their capacity for empathy.

Their inability to experience emotional empathy means that they may not recognize or fully understand the emotions, needs, or suffering of those around them. They may struggle to show compassion or respond appropriately to the emotions of others. This lack of empathy can manifest in various ways, such as disregarding others' feelings, exploiting or manipulating others for personal gain, or displaying a sense of entitlement.

It is important to note that the lack of empathy in narcissists is not necessarily a conscious choice or intentional cruelty. Rather, it is a characteristic that stems from their coping mechanism and the limited emotional development resulting from their traumatic experiences.

Understanding this can help victims of narcissistic abuse recognize that the narcissist's behavior is not a reflection of their worth or deservingness of empathy, but rather a limitation within the narcissist. Empathy plays a crucial role in healthy relationships, emotional connections, and social interactions.

When victims of narcissistic abuse encounter a lack of empathy from the narcissist, it can be deeply distressing and exacerbate their suffering. It is important for victims to recognize that the narcissist's lack of empathy is not their fault and to seek support and healing from the effects of the abuse.

- **Grandiosity:** Narcissistic grandiosity is a core feature of individuals with Narcissistic Personality Disorder (NPD). It represents an exaggerated sense of self-importance and superiority. A narcissist with grandiose tendencies believes himself/herself to be exceptional, unique, and deserving of special treatment and recognition. They view themselves as being above others and expect others to acknowledge and admire their supposed greatness.

This inflated self-image is often accompanied by fantasies of unlimited success, power, beauty, or ideal love, where they envision themselves achieving extraordinary feats and being adored by all. The manifestation of narcissistic grandiosity can be observed in their behaviors and attitudes.

They constantly seek validation and admiration from others, craving attention and recognition to validate their self-worth. They may engage in self-promotion, bragging, or dominating conversations to ensure that the focus remains on them and their perceived greatness.

Belittling others and exploiting them for personal gain is not uncommon, as they view others as mere instruments to serve their own needs and desires. Ultimately, narcissistic grandiosity reflects an inflated self-image that seeks constant reinforcement from external sources, fuelling their need for attention and adulation.

- **Fantasies of unlimited success:** Fantasies of unlimited success are a common aspect of narcissistic grandiosity. Narcissists with these fantasies have an exaggerated and unrealistic belief in their abilities and potential for achievement. They create elaborate scenarios in their minds where they envision themselves attaining extraordinary levels of success, power, wealth, or recognition.

These fantasies serve as a way for them to boost their self-esteem and maintain a sense of superiority over others. In their minds, they are special and destined for greatness, far surpassing the achievements of ordinary individuals. Within these fantasies, narcissists often imagine themselves as exceptional beings who are adored, admired, and envied by others.

They may envision themselves in positions of authority, surrounded by an entourage of followers or achieving remarkable feats that set them apart from the rest of society.

These fantasies provide a temporary escape from their underlying feelings of insecurity and inadequacy. However, it's important to note that these fantasies rarely translate into tangible achievements in reality, as they often lack the motivation, dedication, and willingness to put in the necessary effort to turn their grandiose visions into actual accomplishments.

- **Need for Admiration:** The need for admiration is a fundamental characteristic of narcissistic individuals. It refers to their intense desire for excessive praise, attention, and recognition from others. Narcissists have an insatiable craving to be admired and validated, as it serves to reinforce their inflated self-image and fragile self-esteem.

They rely heavily on external sources to affirm their worth and superiority, seeking constant reassurance that they are special and deserving of admiration.

Narcissists often go to great lengths to gain admiration from others. They may engage in self-promotion, boasting about their achievements, talents, or possessions, in an attempt to elicit admiration and envy. They seek out situations in which they can be the centre of attention, constantly seeking validation through compliments, flattery, and attention from others.

The need for admiration also ties into their need for control and power, as they feel a sense of entitlement to be admired and treated as exceptional. However, despite their relentless pursuit of admiration, it is often short-lived and unsatisfying, as their insatiable need for validation can never be fully met.

- **Interpersonal exploitation:** Interpersonal exploitation is a characteristic behavior commonly observed in individuals with narcissistic personality disorder. It refers to their tendency to manipulate and take advantage of others for their gain or advantage, without regard for the well-being or feelings of those they exploit. Narcissists view others as tools or resources to be used to meet their own needs, desires, or ambitions.

Narcissists excel in identifying and exploiting vulnerabilities in others. They may exploit people's emotions, trust, or dependency on them for their benefit. They often engage in manipulative tactics such as deception, charm, or flattery to gain control and extract what they want from others. This can include exploiting their relationships, professional connections, or financial resources. They lack empathy and remorse, showing little concern for the negative impact their actions may have on those they exploit.

Interpersonal exploitation serves to bolster their grandiose self-image and maintain a sense of superiority. It reflects their deep-seated belief that they are entitled to exploit others without consequence. However, their exploitative behavior often leads to damaged relationships, as people may eventually recognize their manipulative tactics and distance themselves from the narcissist.

- **Enviousness of others:** Enviousness of others is a common trait observed in individuals with Narcissistic Personality Disorder. Narcissists often experience intense feelings of envy towards others, particularly when they perceive others as achieving success, recognition, or possessing qualities that they desire for themselves. This envy stems from their deep-seated insecurity and fragile self-esteem, as they constantly compare themselves to others and feel threatened by the accomplishments and strengths of those around them.

Narcissists have an incessant need to be seen as superior and exceptional, and when they witness others achieving success or receiving admiration, it triggers feelings of inadequacy and a fear of being overshadowed. They may feel a strong sense of entitlement and believe that they should be the ones receiving the attention, admiration, and rewards. As a result, they experience envy towards those they perceive as more successful, attractive, talented, or accomplished.

This envy often leads narcissists to engage in behaviors such as undermining or devaluing others' achievements, engaging in covert competition, or even sabotaging others' success. They may engage in gossip, spreading rumours, or engaging in smear campaigns to diminish the image of those they envy. Envious narcissists struggle with empathizing with others' successes and instead harbour resentment, jealousy, and a desire to regain the spotlight for themselves.

However, their envy ultimately perpetuates a cycle of dissatisfaction, as they are unable to find genuine contentment or fulfilment due to their constant comparison and envy towards others.

- **Need for Status and Attention:** The need for status and attention is a prominent aspect of narcissistic individuals. They have a strong desire to be perceived as important, influential, and superior to others. This need for status and attention stems from their deep-seated insecurity and the belief that their self-worth is tied to external validation.

Narcissists constantly seek positions, achievements, or possessions that elevate their social standing and grant them a sense of superiority. They crave recognition and adulation, often going to great lengths to obtain it. They may pursue high-status careers, engage in self-promotion, or surround themselves with people they perceive as prestigious or influential in order to enhance their own image.

Their need for attention is fuelled by a constant desire to be the centre of focus. They seek admiration, praise, and validation from others, as it reinforces their self-esteem and reinforces their belief in their exceptional qualities. They often engage in attention-seeking behaviors, such as boasting, exaggerating their accomplishments, or seeking out situations where they can be the centre of attention.

The need for status and attention in narcissists is closely tied to their fragile self-esteem. Without constant validation and recognition, they may feel a sense of worthlessness or inadequacy. However, this constant pursuit of status and attention often leads to shallow and superficial relationships, as their focus is primarily on themselves and their own needs, rather than genuine connections with others.

- **Arrogance and Haughtiness:** Arrogance and haughtiness are common traits exhibited by individuals with narcissistic tendencies. These traits are characterized by an exaggerated sense of self-importance, superiority, and a condescending attitude toward others.

Arrogance is the manifestation of an inflated self-view where narcissists believe they are superior to others in various aspects. They often display a sense of entitlement, expecting special treatment, privileges, or recognition due to their perceived exceptional qualities or accomplishments. Arrogant individuals may dismiss the opinions, achievements, or perspectives of others, considering them to be inferior or irrelevant compared to their own.

Haughtiness is closely linked to arrogance and is characterized by an attitude of disdain or contempt towards those whom individuals perceive as beneath them. Individuals with narcissistic traits often exhibit a sense of haughtiness by projecting an air of superiority and treating others with condescension. They may belittle or dismiss the abilities, achievements, or social status of others.".

Arrogance and haughtiness serve as defence mechanisms for narcissists to mask their deep-rooted insecurities and maintain a sense of control and superiority. However, these traits often create interpersonal barriers, alienating others and hindering meaningful connections. The condescending attitude and disregard for others' perspectives contribute to strained relationships and a lack of genuine empathy or mutual respect.

- **Sense of Entitlement:** A sense of entitlement is a key characteristic of narcissistic individuals. It refers to their belief that they deserve special treatment, privileges, or recognition without necessarily having earned or warranted them. Narcissists have an inflated view of their own importance and believe that they are inherently entitled to preferential treatment or benefits.

Individuals with a sense of entitlement often have unrealistic expectations of others and feel a strong sense of deservingness. They may expect others to cater to their needs, fulfil their demands, or prioritize their desires above others'. They may believe that rules or social norms do not apply to them and may try to bend or break them to suit their agenda.

This sense of entitlement is rooted in narcissists' grandiose self-perception and the belief that they are inherently more special or deserving than others. They may feel entitled to admiration, attention, success, or material possessions. This entitlement can manifest in various aspects of their lives, such as personal relationships, professional environments, or social interactions.

This often leads narcissists to exploit others, disregard boundaries, and display a lack of empathy. They may manipulate or use people to achieve their own goals without considering the impact on others' well-being or needs. This entitlement-driven behavior can strain relationships, as it fosters a self-centred mindset that overlooks the perspectives and feelings of others.

"Out of difficulties grow miracles."
Jean de La Bruyère

Chapter Four

Different flavours of Narcissism

While there is no universally agreed-upon classification system for different types of narcissists, some researchers and experts have proposed subtypes or variations based on observable patterns of behavior. These subtypes are not mutually exclusive, and an individual may exhibit traits from multiple subtypes. Here are a few commonly discussed types of narcissists:

- **Grandiose Narcissist:** This is the classic form of narcissism that is characterized by an inflated sense of self-importance, a need for admiration, and a belief in their exceptional abilities. Grandiose narcissists often seek power, success, and dominance over others. They may display arrogance, entitlement, and a disregard for the feelings and needs of others.

- **Vulnerable/Covert Narcissist:** Unlike grandiose narcissists, vulnerable or covert narcissists present themselves as shy, introverted, or even self-deprecating. They often harbour deep feelings of insecurity and have fragile self-esteem. They manipulate others through guilt, self-pity, and a victim mentality, seeking sympathy and attention. They may engage in passive-aggressive behavior and use emotional manipulation to control others.

- **Malignant Narcissist:** Malignant narcissism represents an extreme form of Narcissistic Personality Disorder. It combines the traits of narcissism with antisocial, sadistic, and paranoid behaviors. Malignant narcissists can be highly destructive and may have a callous disregard for the rights and well-being of others. They may engage in exploitative, manipulative, and even aggressive behaviors.

- **Somatic Narcissist:** Somatic narcissists primarily focus on their physical appearance and attractiveness. They derive their self-worth from their physical attributes and use their looks to gain attention and admiration. They often engage in excessive grooming, pursue cosmetic enhancements, and use their physical appearance as a means of seduction and control.

- **Cerebral Narcissist:** Cerebral narcissists emphasize their intellectual superiority and seek validation through their intelligence, knowledge, and accomplishments. They believe they are intellectually superior to others and may engage in intellectual one-upmanship. They use their intellect as a means of asserting dominance and control over others.

"Narcissism Has No Face" is the book title chosen to emphasize that narcissism can manifest in anyone, regardless of background or profession. While certain character traits may be similar among narcissists, they can also exhibit unique variations based on factors such as the severity of their condition and their environment. Let us now explore some similarities and some different flavours of narcissism as it relates to different professions and societal statuses.

Characteristics of a Malignant Narcissist

The term "malignant narcissist" is often used to describe an individual who exhibits the most extreme and dangerous traits of narcissism. Malignant narcissism is not a formal psychiatric diagnosis. It is a descriptive term used to highlight the particularly harmful and destructive behavior seen in some individuals with narcissistic traits.

I much rather refer to the DSM5 when it comes to the severity of the manifestation of these characteristics. But it is a term that is used by many to explain the gravity of their situation. Here are some traits associated with malignant narcissism:

- **Sadism:** Malignant narcissists derive pleasure from causing others pain and may display sadistic tendencies.

- **Manipulation:** They are highly skilled at manipulating and exploiting others to achieve their goals and maintain control over them.

- **Lack of Empathy:** Malignant narcissists lack genuine empathy and are often unable to understand or care about the suffering of others.

- **Extreme Grandiosity:** They have an exaggerated sense of self-importance and believe they are superior to others in every way.

- **Paranoia:** Malignant narcissists may be extremely paranoid and see others as threats to their sense of self or power.

- **Pathological Lies:** They may engage in frequent and compulsive lying to maintain their self-image and manipulate others.

- **Narcissistic Rages:** Malignant narcissists can display explosive rages when their grandiose self-image is threatened or when they feel slighted or criticized.

- **Antisocial Behavior:** They may disregard social norms and laws, engaging in exploitative and harmful behaviors without remorse.

- **Lack of Morals or Ethics:** Malignant narcissists often act with complete disregard for ethical principles or the well-being of others.

- **Predatory Behavior:** They may target vulnerable individuals for exploitation and take pleasure in dominating and controlling them, even to the point of stalking.

- **Triangulation:** Malignant narcissists may create conflicts and divisions among others to maintain their control and power over social situations.

It is essential to recognize that dealing with a malignant narcissist can be extremely challenging and even dangerous, as their lack of empathy and potential for aggressive behaviors can have severe consequences for those around them.

If you suspect that someone in your life may exhibit malignant narcissistic traits, it is crucial to seek support from mental health professionals and consider implementing safety measures to protect yourself and others from potential harm.

The Overt vs the Covert Narcissist

I've heard many mentions of the overt and the covert narcissist, I now define the differences in both such flavours of narcissism for ease of reference:

The Overt Narcissist

- **Visibility:** Overt narcissists display their narcissistic traits openly and seek attention and admiration from others. They want to be noticed and often engage in attention-seeking behaviors to be the center of attention.

- **Grandiosity:** They have an inflated sense of self-importance and believe they are special, unique, and superior to others. Their grandiosity is evident in their behavior and speech.

- **Boastful and Arrogant:** Overt narcissists frequently boast about their accomplishments, talents, or possessions, and they may come across as arrogant or condescending.

- **Lack of Empathy:** They have difficulty understanding or caring about others' feelings and needs. Empathy is generally lacking in their interactions with others.

- **Boundary Violations:** Overt narcissists may disregard others' boundaries and act in ways that are intrusive or disrespectful.

Covert Narcissist

Hidden Behaviors: Covert narcissists display their narcissistic traits in more subtle and hidden ways. They may not overtly seek attention or praise but still have an underlying sense of entitlement and self-importance.

- **Victim Mentality:** Covert narcissists often adopt a victim mentality, portraying themselves as misunderstood, unappreciated, or mistreated to elicit sympathy and attention from others.

- **Low Self-Esteem:** Despite their sense of superiority, covert narcissists may have low self-esteem and use their grandiosity as a defence mechanism to protect themselves from feelings of inadequacy.

- **Passive-Aggressive Behavior:** They may engage in passive-aggressive behavior, such as making snide remarks or using sarcasm, to indirectly express their displeasure or manipulate others.

- **Sensitive to Criticism:** Covert narcissists may be especially sensitive to criticism and may react defensively or withdraw emotionally when their flaws or mistakes are pointed out.

- **Empathy as a Manipulative Tool:** Covert narcissists may use feigned empathy to manipulate others and gain their trust, only to later exploit their vulnerabilities.

While overt and covert narcissists may display different behaviors, both types share the core characteristics of narcissism, such as a lack of empathy, an excessive need for admiration, and a sense of entitlement.

SUE BARKER

Understanding the differences between overt and covert narcissism can help in recognizing and dealing with these individuals in personal and professional relationships. However, it is important to remember that diagnosing and dealing with personality disorders like narcissism should be left to qualified mental health professionals.

The Narcissistic Parent

Narcissistic parents exhibit a range of behaviors that can have a significant impact on their children. Their behaviors can vary in severity and manifestation. There are some traits in the parent narcissist that can also be similar to that of the regular narcissist. That's because narcissism does not discriminate when it comes to protecting the afflicted one.

It will adopt manipulative tactics to achieve the agenda, at any cost necessary from the victim, whether their child or anyone they set their eye on.

As you examine the traits of a narcissistic parent, keep in mind that that parent is also the partner of someone who may very well be a victim in the scheme of things. Here are some of the traits:

- **Grandiosity and self-centeredness:** Narcissistic parents often display an exaggerated sense of self-importance and prioritize their own needs and desires above those of their children. They may constantly seek admiration and attention from their children.

- **Lack of empathy:** Narcissistic parents are often self-absorbed and lack empathy. Empaths tend to desire validation and love from a narcissist, potentially due to their childhood experience of not having their emotional needs met by a caregiver or parent. Likely, an empath had a narcissistic parent or experienced some kind of emotional neglect in which they learned that love is conditional.

In a narcissistic family, the parent's needs take precedence over the children. Although children of a narcissist aren't shown empathy by their parents, they are nonetheless expected to demonstrate empathy to that parent and to relieve the parent's feelings of insecurity or vulnerability.

- **Emotional manipulation and control:** Narcissistic parents use emotional manipulation and control tactics to maintain power and dominance over their children. They may use guilt, gaslighting, or emotional blackmail to shape their children's behavior and maintain their sense of superiority.

- **Parentification or infantilization:** Narcissistic parents may reverse the typical parent-child roles by making their children responsible for their emotional well-being or relying on them for support, referred to as parentification. Alternatively, they may treat their children as extensions of themselves, infantilizing them and not allowing them to develop autonomy or independence.

- **Golden child/scapegoat dynamics:** Narcissistic parents may engage in favouritism, designating one child as the "golden child" and the other as the "scapegoat." The golden child is idealized, while the scapegoat is subjected to blame, criticism, and punishment, creating a toxic dynamic between the siblings.

- **Boundary violations:** Narcissistic parents may have poor respect for boundaries, invading their children's privacy or using them as extensions of themselves. They may not recognize or respect their children's individuality, personal space, or autonomy.

- **Emotional and verbal abuse:** Narcissistic parents may engage in emotional and verbal abuse, including insults, humiliation, belittlement, or constant criticism. They may use these tactics to maintain control, diminish their children's self-esteem, or ensure compliance.

- **Unpredictable and inconsistent behavior:** Narcissistic parents can be unpredictable in their moods and behaviors, creating an unstable and chaotic environment for their children. They may alternate between love and affection and anger or rejection, leaving their children feeling anxious and uncertain.

- **Lack of genuine parental support:** Narcissistic parents may be unable or unwilling to provide consistent emotional support, guidance, or nurturing to their children. They may view their children as objects to fulfil their own needs rather than as individuals with unique needs and emotions.

However, it's important to recognize that individuals can heal and grow despite the challenges they faced in their upbringing. With the right support, therapy, and self-work, adult survivors of narcissistic abuse can develop resilience, regain their self-worth, and create healthier relationships. Seeking therapy or counselling specifically tailored for this type of abuse can be beneficial, for both adult survivors and children of narcissistic parents. It provides a safe space to process the trauma, gain understanding, and learn healthy coping mechanisms and relationship skills.

The Political Narcissist

The term "Political Narcissist" refers to individuals who exhibit narcissistic traits or behaviors within the realm of politics. Political narcissism is characterized by an excessive preoccupation with oneself, a grandiose sense of self-importance, a lack of empathy, a need for admiration, and a tendency to exploit others for personal gain. Here are some key aspects and implications of political narcissism:

*   **Grandiosity and Self-Importance:** Political narcissists often have an inflated sense of their importance and abilities. They may believe they are uniquely qualified or destined for positions of power and authority. This grandiose self-perception drives their desire for recognition, admiration, and control.

*   **Lack of Empathy:** Political narcissists tend to lack empathy and have difficulty understanding or caring about the needs and concerns of others. They may prioritize their interests and agendas above the well-being of the people they are supposed to serve. This can lead to policies and decisions that prioritize personal gain or self-preservation rather than the greater good.

*   **Exploitative Behaviors:** Political narcissists may manipulate and exploit others to further their agenda. They may use charm, charisma, and manipulation tactics to gain support and loyalty from others. They may also engage in deceitful or unethical practices to maintain power and control.

*   **Image Management and Self-Promotion:** Political narcissists are often highly focused on managing their public image and promoting themselves. They may engage in self-aggrandizement, exaggeration of achievements, and selective

presentation of information to enhance their image and gain public support.

Lack of Accountability: Political narcissists may display a sense of entitlement and resist taking responsibility for their actions. They may deflect blame onto others, deny wrongdoing, or distort facts to protect their image and maintain their position of power.

Fragile Self-Esteem: Despite their outward display of confidence and superiority, political narcissists may have fragile self-esteem that is easily threatened by criticism or perceived slights. They may react defensively or aggressively when their actions or policies are challenged or questioned.

It is important to note that not all politicians exhibit narcissistic traits and that political narcissism, like all others exists on a spectrum. However, when individuals with narcissistic tendencies hold positions of power in politics, it can have significant implications for governance, decision-making, and the well-being of citizens.

Awareness of political narcissism can help foster a more informed and discerning electorate. It is crucial to critically evaluate politicians based on their actions, integrity, empathy, and commitment to public service rather than being swayed solely by charisma or grandiose promises. Holding political leaders accountable for their behavior and promoting ethical leadership can contribute to a healthier and more functional political system.

The Narcissistic Employer

A Narcissistic Employer refers to a boss or manager who displays narcissistic traits or exhibits narcissistic behavior patterns within the workplace. These individuals prioritize their own needs, desires, and self-aggrandizement over the well-being and success of their employees or the organization as a whole. Here are some characteristics and behaviors commonly associated with a narcissistic employer played out in the story below.

In a bustling city of Port of Spain, there was a thriving company called Company X. At the helm of this company was a charismatic and ambitious CEO named Richard. To the outside world, Richard was seen as a successful and visionary leader, but within the walls of the company, his true narcissistic nature emerged.

Richard revelled in his position of power and took pleasure in asserting his dominance over his employees. He saw them as mere instruments to fuel his ego and advance his agenda. He craved constant admiration and sought to maintain an atmosphere of fear and control.

Under Richard's leadership, the workplace became a toxic environment. He would belittle and demean his employees, using manipulation and gaslighting to undermine their self-confidence. He exploited their talents and accomplishments, taking credit for their work while disregarding their contributions.

One of the employees, Cheryl, was particularly targeted by Richard's narcissistic tendencies. As a talented and dedicated professional, Cheryl became a threat to Richard's fragile ego. He went to great lengths to undermine her achievements, constantly criticizing her work and sabotaging her chances of advancement.

Despite the toxic atmosphere, Cheryl refused to let Richard's behavior crush her spirit. She sought support from her colleagues, sharing their stories of similar experiences. Together, they formed a support network, empowering each other to stand up against the narcissistic employer.

Driven by a shared desire for change, the employees decided to take action. They meticulously documented instances of Richard's abusive behavior and sought legal advice. They also anonymously reported the toxic work environment to higher authorities, ensuring that their voices were heard.

As the truth about Richard's narcissism and abuse of power began to surface, the company faced a reckoning. Public scrutiny mounted, tarnishing the company's reputation and forcing the board of directors to take action. Richard's true colours were exposed, and he was eventually removed from his position as CEO.

With Richard's departure, a new era of healing and growth began at Company X. The employees came together to rebuild the company culture, promoting transparency, respect, and collaboration. They implemented policies to protect employees from narcissistic abuse and fostered a supportive work environment.

Cheryl, now empowered and resilient, became a catalyst for change within the company. She took on a leadership role, advocating for employee well-being and ensuring that no one would experience the horrors of a narcissistic employer again.

The story of Company X serves as a cautionary tale about the damaging effects of narcissism in the workplace. It highlights the importance of recognizing and addressing toxic behaviors, as well as the resilience and collective strength of employees in standing up against abuse.

While the case of Richard the CEO is utilized as an illustrative example, it's important to note that such situations are not unique.

It is a proven fact that people who suffer from NPD often pursue careers where they can be in control. They usually abuse that power to gain narcissistic fuel as described below:

Narcissistic employers often have an inflated sense of self-worth and believe they are superior to others. They may exaggerate their accomplishments, demand constant praise and admiration, and expect special treatment from their employees. They struggle to empathize with their employees' experiences, emotions, and needs.

They may show little concern for their employees' well-being and may be dismissive of their problems or concerns. Narcissistic employers may exploit their employees for their gain. They may manipulate situations to maintain power and control, using tactics such as favouritism, gaslighting, or playing employees against each other.

Narcissistic employers often have a strong need for control and may micromanage their employees' work, undermining their autonomy and confidence. They may impose unrealistic expectations, set arbitrary rules, and closely monitor every aspect of their employees' performance.

Listed below are some characteristics that can help to identify narcissism in the workplace for ease of reference:

- Inflated self-worth and superiority complex
- Exaggeration of accomplishments and constant need for praise and admiration
- Lack of empathy and disregard for employees' experiences, emotions, and needs
- Exploitation of employees for personal gain

- Manipulative tactics such as favouritism, gaslighting, and playing employees against each other
- Strong need for control and micromanagement of employees' work
- Imposition of unrealistic expectations and arbitrary rules
- Closely monitoring and undermining employees' autonomy and confidence.

These traits collectively illustrate the toxic and destructive nature of a narcissistic employer within the workplace. Their actions create a toxic environment, undermine employee well-being, and hinder the overall success of the organization. Recognizing and addressing these narcissistic behaviors is crucial for fostering a healthy and supportive work culture.

Due to their demanding and exploitative behavior, narcissistic employers often experience high employee turnover and increased levels of burnout. The negative impact on employee morale and job satisfaction can be significant.

Dealing with a narcissistic employer can be challenging for employees. It is important for employees to set boundaries, maintain their self-worth, and seek support from colleagues, mentors, or HR departments if necessary. Recognizing the signs of narcissistic behavior and understanding strategies for self-preservation can help employees navigate the workplace and protect their well-being.

Disclaimer: The stories shared are for illustrative purposes only. Any semblance of actual stories is purely coincidental

The Narcissistic Friend

A Narcissistic Friend refers to an individual who exhibits narcissistic traits or behaviors within a friendship. These individuals prioritize their own needs, seek constant validation and admiration, are usually envious, and often lack empathy or consideration for the feelings and needs of others. Once you know what to look for, they can be very easy to spot.

One such example can be this. You may have a friend who only dresses after they see what you're wearing and they try to out-dress you. Or, they may ill speak your mate or other friends in their absence but when the individual is present, their attitude toward that person is totally the opposite. Here are some characteristics and behaviors commonly associated with a narcissistic friend:

- **Self-centeredness:** Narcissistic friends tend to be excessively self-focused and show little interest in others' lives or experiences. They may dominate conversations, steer topics back to themselves, and expect others to always prioritize their needs and desires.

- **Need for admiration:** Narcissistic friends crave constant validation and admiration from others. They may seek compliments, flattery, and attention, and may become upset or resentful if they feel they are not receiving enough praise or admiration.

- **Lack of empathy:** Narcissistic friends often struggle to genuinely empathize with others. They may be dismissive of others' emotions or problems, show little concern for their friends' well-being, and struggle to provide support or understanding in times of need.

- **Exploitation and manipulation:** Narcissistic friends may exploit their friendships for personal gain. They may use their friends for their benefit, such as seeking favours, using them as a sounding board for their problems, or expecting constant attention and support without reciprocating.

- **Boundary violations:** Narcissistic friends may disregard personal boundaries and exhibit controlling or invasive behavior. They may disregard or dismiss their friends' boundaries, invade their privacy, or pressure them into doing things with which they are uncomfortable.

- **Jealousy and competition:** Narcissistic friends may be prone to jealousy and competition with their friends. They may feel threatened by their friends' successes or accomplishments and may try to undermine or diminish them to maintain a sense of superiority.

- **Lack of reciprocity:** Narcissistic friends often have difficulty offering genuine support, listening, or being there for others. They may only be interested in conversations or activities that revolve around them, and may not provide the same level of emotional support or care in return.

Dealing with a narcissistic friend can be challenging and emotionally draining. It is important to establish and enforce healthy boundaries, communicate your needs clearly, and evaluate whether the friendship is beneficial and supportive for your well-being.

If the friendship becomes toxic or consistently detrimental, it may be necessary to distance yourself or end the friendship for your own emotional health, happiness and peace of mind.

However, always keep in mind that diagnosis and treatment should be conducted by qualified mental health professionals based on a comprehensive evaluation of an individual's symptoms and circumstances.

Narcissism and Religious Leaders

From my research on the topic of narcissism, I've come to realize that narcissism exists in every aspect of our lives. It is the main reason I embarked on this journey to bring awareness to you in as much detail as possible in my book. We'll now take a look at narcissism from the aspect of the religious leader:

In the small town of Clearwater, nestled among rolling hills, there was a charismatic and influential religious leader named Reverend Matthew. With a captivating presence and a gift for persuasive speaking, he attracted a devoted following to his church, The Graceful Path.

Reverend Matthew, however, had a sinister side masked by his divine persona. Behind closed doors, he revelled in the power and adoration bestowed upon him by his congregation. He used his position of authority to manipulate and control those who sought spiritual guidance and solace.

One of the parishioners, Emily, was drawn to Reverend Matthew's magnetic personality and his promises of salvation. She yearned for meaning and guidance in her life, and she believed he held the answers. Little did she know that Reverend Matthew's intentions were far from genuine.

As Emily became more involved in the church, Reverend Matthew began to exploit her vulnerability. He strategically showered her with compliments and attention, making her feel special and chosen among the congregation. He used her devotion as a means to inflate his ego and maintain his control.

Under the guise of providing spiritual counsel, Reverend Matthew manipulated Emily's thoughts and emotions. He convinced her that she was uniquely connected to the divine and that her purpose was to serve him and the church unquestioningly. Emily became entangled in a web of psychological manipulation, her self-esteem and critical thinking eroded by Reverend Matthew's gaslighting.

Behind the scenes, Reverend Matthew was living a life of opulence, indulging in luxuries funded by the generous donations of his followers. He exploited their faith and trust, using their hard-earned money to support his lavish lifestyle while preaching about humility and sacrifice.

As rumours and whispers began to circulate within the congregation about Reverend Matthew's true nature, some members started to question his teachings and actions. A small group of courageous individuals, disillusioned by his hypocrisy, started gathering evidence of his deceptive practices.

With undeniable proof in hand, the group confronted Reverend Matthew, demanding accountability for his manipulative behavior and financial misconduct. The truth was revealed, causing shockwaves throughout the church community. Members who had once idolized him were left shattered and betrayed.

In the aftermath, the church community began the long process of healing and rebuilding. They sought solace in one another's support, re-evaluating their beliefs and reassessing the true essence of faith. Together, they are working to create a more inclusive and transparent spiritual environment, free from the influence of narcissistic leaders.

Reverend Matthew's story serves as a cautionary example, illustrating how narcissism can infiltrate even the most sacred spaces. It underscores the importance of remaining vigilant and questioning authority, as well as the resilience of individuals coming together to expose the truth and reclaim their spiritual journeys.

Sadly, we have a lot of Reverend Matthew in our midst today. Narcissism seems to have our world under siege as we can see the effects of it all around us. Some of the characteristics of narcissism manifested in this story are as follows:

- Charismatic presence and persuasive speaking abilities
- Excessive need for adoration and power
- Manipulation and control of followers
- Exploitation of vulnerabilities for personal gain
- Gaslighting and manipulation of thoughts and emotions
- Living a life of opulence while preaching about humility and sacrifice
- Hypocrisy and deceitful practices
- Lack of accountability for manipulative behavior and financial misconduct.

Although this is an illustrative story it is sad to say that we do have a lot of Reverend Matthew in our midst today.

Disclaimer: The stories shared are for illustrative purposes only. Any semblance to actual stories is purely coincidental

The Narcissist in the Military

Individuals with Narcissistic Personality Disorder (NPD) may be drawn to joining the military for various reasons. However, please note that not everyone who chooses that career path is narcissistic. However, reports have shown, that there is a high percentage of individuals affected with the traits, due to the dynamics of the environment. These are some characteristics that can manifest in individuals that are so inclined:

- **Leadership Dynamics:** In military settings, narcissistic leaders may prioritize their self-interests over the well-being of their subordinates. They may seek personal glory, crave excessive admiration, and exploit their position of power. This can create a toxic work environment, erode trust, and hinder effective teamwork.

- **Manipulation and Exploitation:** Narcissistic individuals may exploit the dedication and loyalty of soldiers for personal gain. They may use their influence to manipulate others, gain preferential treatment, or secure personal achievements at the expense of the unit or mission. This can lead to resentment, frustration, and a breakdown of morale among soldiers.

- **Emotional and Psychological Impact:** Soldiers who serve under narcissistic leaders may experience emotional and psychological distress. Constant criticism, belittlement, and unrealistic expectations can take a toll on their self-esteem and mental well-being. The constant need for validation and praise from a narcissistic leader can create an unhealthy and stressful environment.

- **Unrealistic Expectations:** Narcissistic leaders may set unrealistic goals or demand unwavering loyalty without considering the practical limitations and well-being of their soldiers. This can lead to burnout, increased stress levels, and a sense of disillusionment among the troops.

- **Limited Room for Growth**: Narcissistic leaders often prioritize their advancement and may be reluctant to promote or recognize the achievements of their subordinates. This can hinder the professional growth and development of soldiers, leading to frustration and a lack of motivation.

Although, not all leaders in the military may exhibit narcissistic traits, a report from Medscape.com stated that, "NPD is found in 6% of the forensic population, and in 5 out of 6 or 20% of the military population," The impact of narcissism can vary depending on the specific circumstances and individuals involved. However, when narcissistic behavior is present within the military, it can have detrimental effects on the well-being and cohesion of soldiers and the overall effectiveness of the unit.

One historical example of a military leader often characterized as having narcissistic traits is General Douglas MacArthur. MacArthur was a prominent American military figure during the 20th century, serving as a general in World War II and the Korean War.

MacArthur was known for his grandiose self-image and belief in his exceptionalism. He had a strong desire for attention and admiration, often displaying a sense of entitlement and superiority. He sought to cultivate an image of himself as a larger-than-life figure, often portrayed in dramatic and heroic terms.

MacArthur's actions demonstrated his need for control and dominance. He tended to micromanage and exert authority over subordinates, and he was known for his strong-willed and uncompromising leadership style. His decisions, such as his controversial handling of the Korean War and his dismissal by President Truman, reflected General MacArthur's self-assured and grandiose nature.

- **Leadership Dynamics:** Narcissistic leaders prioritize their self-interests, seek personal glory, and exploit their power.

- **Manipulation and Exploitation:** Narcissistic individuals manipulate and exploit the dedication and loyalty of soldiers for personal gain.

- **Emotional and Psychological Impact:** Soldiers under narcissistic leaders may experience constant criticism, belittlement and psychological pressure, leading to emotional distress.

- **Unrealistic Expectations:** Narcissistic leaders set unrealistic goals and demand unwavering loyalty without considering practical limitations.

- **Limited Room for Growth:** Narcissistic leaders prioritize their advancement and hinder the professional growth of subordinates.

- **Presence in Forensic and Military Populations:** Reports indicate a higher prevalence of Narcissistic Personality Disorder in the forensic and military populations, suggesting a significant presence of narcissistic traits in military settings.

It's important to remember that while these traits can be observed in certain military leaders, not all leaders in the military exhibit narcissistic traits. Additionally, diagnosing specific psychological disorders in historical figures is speculative and challenging, but analysing their behavior and leadership style through the lens of narcissistic traits can provide insights into their actions and impact.

"Be grateful for your battles, for they can strengthen you in ways you can't imagine. They will lead you to a strength you never knew you had. Embrace them!"
Sue Barker

Chapter Five

The Retaliation of the Afflicted

There was a story featured in the public domain about a British teenager that brutally murdered his parents in 2004. It was reported that he was under significant pressure from his parents regarding his academic achievements. His mother was unusually controlling to the point of dressing him for school even after he attained the age of seventeen. She even walked him to school every day in view of the neighbours and his friends at school.

To protect his character and save face, this teenager developed a coping mechanism that allowed him to create stories of being a successful tennis player and part owner of his father's business. He managed to convince his mates of this façade which he had to maintain even to the point of his gruesome act toward his parents.

It was reported that on the evening the killings took place the teenager was trying to obtain his father's credit cards. This was for him to follow through with a promise he had made to his girlfriend of a lavish vacation in New York.

As the news of the gruesome killings spread through the global community, it was revealed that the teenager assaulted his father with a hammer, when he refused to yield to his financial wishes.

On seeing the commotion his mother tried to save her husband by grabbing a kitchen knife to challenge her son, but this did not go well for her. The teenager attacked his mother with the same kitchen knife, dealing her multiple stab wounds that eventually caused her demise. After leaving his parents for dead, he proceeded on the planned vacation with his girlfriend, using his father's credit cards while pretending they were his own.

The teenager spent two weeks on this grand vacation, using up his father's credit cards to impress his girlfriend without any remorse for what he had done. Upon returning, the teenager was awarded for his academic achievements which he celebrated with his friends at school. He stayed at a nearby hotel and went about his business like normal with no regard for his parents' dead bodies at home.

After reports were made to the authorities of a terrible stench emanating from the teenager's home, the badly decomposing bodies of his parents were discovered, and the teenager was questioned and evaluated by mental health professionals to determine his mental state.

They were baffled at his calm demeanour despite the tragedy that befell his family. It was also reported that neighbours were interviewed and commented on the less-than-normal behavior of his mother who seemed to idealize the teenager. He was her only child and she accompanied him almost everywhere.

Investigations continued, but it was not until a few months after the murders that he was arrested on suspicion. During police interviews, the teenager admitted killing his parents but said it was "a split-second thing" and, "I just couldn't believe what I'd done".

He told investigators that before his father died, he went over and held his hand and talked to him for a while, telling him he still loved him. Shocked neighbours described him as a lovely, quiet, and clever young man, who played tennis and studied hard.

Nine months after his arrest, the teenager's trial began. Due to the dynamics of the case, it was presided over by a judge, a prosecutor and a team of five psychiatrists.

As the story continued the teenager wrote a letter which was presented to the court which read as follows, "For every moment of every day I wish I could turn back the hands of time. I eternally long to be a little boy again at a time when everyone loved each other, when we could have a happy time and be a family once more...I miss them more than anything in the world. The guilt will punish and haunt me for 24 hours a day for the rest of my life."

In an attempt to find a motive for the killings, it was suggested that the teenager's parents may have discovered his plans to holiday in America with his girlfriend and tried to stop him. This may have induced a rage that drove him to murder.

One of the main points to note here is that the behavior of the narcissist is not premeditated. Their instinctive behavior can be seen as a pattern that is manifested throughout their cycles of behavior. This is because the false personality that arrests and imprisons the true self defends them at all costs. It takes on any role necessary no matter the consequences.

After an extensive examination, it was unanimously agreed that the teenager had narcissistic personality disorder (NPD). People with this disorder typically fantasize about unlimited brilliance, power, and success and often fly into an inappropriate rage if their fantasies are challenged or threatened.

Narcissists are very selfish, with a strong sense of entitlement, needing constantly to be praised and treated like royalty by everyone. The reason NPD sufferers are so convincing to others is that part of them believes their inflated fantasies themselves.

One psychiatrist described the teenager as "a highly abnormal young man", adding that an NPD diagnosis was unusual for someone of his age. He also stated that there was nothing to indicate that the murders were premeditated.

It was noted that there was only evidence to attest to the fact that the teenager's parents were loving and supportive of him. Due to his suffering from severe NPD, and even though, these days, cases of 'diminished responsibility' are extremely rare, the Judge accepted the plea to drop the charges of murder in favour of manslaughter.

The Judge added that, in his opinion, the teenager would never be fit for release. He was convicted and is currently serving a life sentence for the murders. He could not be given the death penalty because he was still a juvenile at the time of the incident.

What I found quite fascinating was when he said he didn't know what happened. It all happened so fast, yet he was able to go about his business as normal.

The characteristics of NPD manifested in this true story are as follows:

- **Pathological lying:** The teenager was known to fabricate extravagant stories about his accomplishments and lifestyle, such as being a professional tennis player and partnering with his father in business.

- **Grandiosity:** He had a tendency towards grandiose fantasies, seeking admiration and recognition for achievements that were not based in reality.

Lack of empathy: The teenager showed no concern after killing his both parents and proceeding on vacation as if nothing had happened. He also returned with no concern about the dead bodies that he had left at his home. Instead, he attended his awards and conducted other business unrelated to the murder of his parents.

- **Impulsivity and aggression:** The teenager exhibited impulsive and violent behavior, brutally assaulting and ultimately killing both of his parents in a fit of rage.

- **Exploitation:** He manipulated his girlfriend and others around him convincing them of his extravagant lifestyle for his gain.

- **Lack of remorse:** Despite the heinous nature of his crimes, the teenager showed limited remorse, celebrating his academic achievements and going on vacation while his parents' bodies remained at home.

- **Sense of entitlement:** He felt entitled to his parents' financial resources, engaging in fraudulent behavior and expecting others to cater to his needs and desires.

- **Delusions of grandeur:** The teenager fantasized about an idealized past where everyone loved each other and longed to be a child again, implying a distorted sense of self-importance and a desire for special status within the family.

Although the teenager's story is indeed a horrific one, not all stories of narcissism exhibit such extreme severity as in this case. Narcissism exists on a spectrum, ranging from mild to severe.

While some individuals may display narcissistic traits that cause significant harm to themselves and others, others may exhibit milder forms of narcissism that are less destructive.

It is important to recognize the varying degrees of narcissism and understand that not all individuals with narcissistic traits will engage in extreme or violent behavior like the teenager did. Stories like this have been noticeably making headlines over the years. Mental illnesses or psychological imbalances conceal themselves in a lot of these stories.

The awareness allows us to recognize personality disorders and their traits to keep us on guard to avoid possible harm or falling victim to their destructive tendencies. By shining a spotlight on these narratives, we gain insight into the complexities of human behavior so we can stay alert. We can also use our knowledge to help those that are affected by recommending professional help at an early stage.

Empathy, knowledge and understanding are key ingredients while we're on this path. Moreover, these stories underscore the importance of early detection and proper support systems, highlighting the significance of mental health awareness in our society.

Through these tales, we're reminded of the need to nurture a compassionate and informed community that can recognize and address the challenges posed by personality disorders. In this way, we can ultimately work towards a safer and more empathetic world for everyone.

Narcissism's Role in Criminal Minds

Narcissism, when present within criminal elements of society, can have significant implications for both the individuals involved and, the communities affected. Certainly, when it comes to criminal elements, not all individuals will display every characteristic associated with narcissism. The presence and severity of certain traits can vary among perpetrators, depending on the individual's specific circumstances and psychological makeup.

Just like narcissism, the manifestation of criminal behavior is influenced by various factors, including the severity of the affliction or disorder present in the individual. It is important to understand that each case is unique, and not all criminal elements will exhibit the same set of characteristics or engage in identical behaviors. Here are some key points to consider when delving into the understanding of the character of the criminals in our society:

- **Manipulation and Exploitation:** Narcissistic individuals may use manipulation tactics to exploit others for personal gain. In criminal contexts, this can manifest as fraud, scams, or even more severe offenses such as identity theft or financial crimes. The narcissistic individual's lack of empathy and disregard for the well-being of others can make them more prone to engaging in illegal activities.

- **Power and Control:** Narcissists often crave power, control, and attention. In criminal behavior, this can lead to acts of violence, aggression, or coercion. For example, individuals with narcissistic traits may engage in domestic violence, sexual assault, or organized crime to assert dominance over others and fulfil their desire for control.

- **Lack of Accountability**: Narcissistic individuals often struggle with taking responsibility for their actions and may deflect blame onto others. This can create a pattern of repeated criminal behavior, as they refuse to acknowledge the harm they cause and continue to engage in illegal activities without remorse.

- **Social Influence:** Narcissists can be charismatic and skilled at influencing others. In criminal settings, they may exploit their charm and persuasive abilities to recruit others into criminal activities or create a following that enables their illicit behavior. This can contribute to the perpetuation of criminal networks and the spread of criminal acts within communities.

- **Resistance to Rehabilitation:** Narcissistic individuals may exhibit resistance to rehabilitation efforts, as they often perceive themselves as superior and beyond reproach. They may resist therapeutic interventions or display a lack of motivation to change their behavior, making it challenging to address the underlying issues contributing to their criminal actions.

Understanding the connection between narcissism and criminal behavior can help us develop strategies for prevention, intervention, and rehabilitation. It is crucial for law enforcement agencies, mental health professionals, and the justice system to work collaboratively in identifying and addressing the underlying factors that contribute to criminal behavior associated with narcissism.

Additionally, raising awareness and promoting social and emotional education can help individuals develop healthy self-esteem and empathy. Whereby, reducing the prevalence of narcissistic traits, and their potential impact on criminal activities in our society

- **Contact and rekindling:** The narcissistic abuser may reach out to the victim, often unexpectedly, after a period of no contact or following a breakup. They may use various means of communication, such as phone calls, text messages, emails, or social media, to initiate contact and attempt to rekindle the relationship.

- **Love bombing:** During the hoovering phase, the narcissistic abuser may revert to the initial love-bombing tactics they used in the early stages of the relationship. They may shower the victim with attention, affection, and promises of change, attempting to reignite feelings of love and attachment.

- **Apologies and remorse:** The abuser may express remorse for their past behavior, acknowledging their wrongdoings and promising to change. They may offer apologies, make promises, and create an illusion of personal growth or transformation to lure the victim back into the relationship.

- **Manipulation and guilt-tripping:** Hoovering often involves manipulation tactics designed to make the victim feel guilty or responsible for the problems in the relationship. The abuser may blame the victim, minimize their abusive behavior, or distort the past to manipulate the victim's emotions and weaken their resolve to leave.

- **Prolonging contact and creating dependency:** The abuser may intentionally prolong contact with the victim, even if the relationship has officially ended. They may create a sense of dependency, making the victim feel that they cannot live without them or that they will never find love elsewhere. This can keep the victim emotionally tied to the abuser and make it more challenging for them to break free.

The narcissist will continue to exert power and control over the victim's emotions, thoughts, and behaviors every time he/she is given the opportunity. The cycle can be extremely damaging to the victim's self-esteem, mental and emotional well-being, and the overall quality of his/her life.

However, not all relationships with narcissists follow this exact cycle, and the severity and duration of each stage may vary. Depending on the degree of narcissism involved. Additionally, leaving an abusive relationship with a narcissist can be challenging. This is due to the manipulative tactics employed by the narcissist to maintain control.

This cycle eventually causes the victim to form a strong attachment with the narcissist. This is fuelled by intermittent reinforcement, where the narcissist alternates between periods of affection and validation and periods of mistreatment. This creates a cycle of hope and despair, further entrenching the victim in the relationship.

Narcissists are Master Manipulators

Whether it's a romantic interest, a parent, a boss, a friend, or a co-worker, there are some tell-tale signs you can look for when dealing with an individual that is suffering from this complex mechanism. Always keep in mind that narcissists are masters at what they do. That's why they are called "Master Manipulators!"

They are usually very charming, patient, seemingly genuine and, extremely cunning. So, you have to be cognizant of the fact that time is an important factor if you have to recognize the games narcissists play. Awareness and discernment should be your best friends at all times.

They possess an uncanny knack for honing in on the weaknesses and insecurities of individuals, allowing them to exploit and manipulate with precision. Just as a vampire is drawn to the life-giving essence of blood, narcissists are instinctively drawn to the emotional vulnerabilities of their targets.

With a calculated and predatory nature, they utilize this knowledge to gain power and control over their victims, feeding off their emotional energy and leaving them drained and depleted. The cycle of behavior is another aspect of the narcissist that you need to pay attention to.

The narcissistic cycle of abuse refers to the recurring pattern of behaviors and dynamics exhibited by a narcissist in any relationship. It typically consists of the following stages:

- **Love bombing:** Love bombing is a manipulative tactic commonly employed by narcissists as part of their seduction or grooming. It involves showering the target individual with excessive affection, attention, compliments, and gifts to quickly establish a deep emotional connection and gain control over them.

Love bombing typically occurs during the initial stages of a relationship or encounter with a narcissist and serves several purposes for the narcissist. However, please note that love bombing is not exclusive to narcissists, and individuals without narcissistic traits can engage in intense displays of affection as well. But love bombing from a narcissist is more intense and overwhelming, so discernment should always be used.

- **Rapid bonding:** Rapid bonding by overwhelming the target with love and affection, the narcissist aims to create an intense emotional bond in a short period. This can make the target feel deeply desired, and valued, fostering a sense of intimacy and trust.

- **Idealization:** Love bombing allows the narcissist to present themselves as the perfect partner often mirroring the target's interests, preferences, and values, creating a false sense of compatibility and shared ideals. The narcissist may praise and idolize the target, making them believe that they have found their ideal mate.

- **Mirroring:** I would expand on mirroring here because this, for me, is the most deceptive stage of a narcissist's cycle of ensnarement. Mirroring is a term often used in the context of narcissistic abuse. It refers to a manipulative technique employed by narcissists to gain control and influence over their victims. In the early stages of a relationship with a narcissist, they often engage in mirroring behaviors to create a false sense of connection and compatibility.

Mirroring involves imitating or reflecting the interests, values, and qualities of their target to establish a bond and gain their trust. They may mimic the victim's likes, dislikes, and even personality traits to create the illusion of shared interests and compatibility.

By mirroring the victim, the narcissist can create a strong emotional connection, making the victim feel understood and validated. This manipulation tactic serves to build a sense of trust and dependency, making the victim more susceptible to the narcissist's influence and control.

However, as the relationship progresses, the narcissist's mirroring behavior tends to fade away. They reveal their true self, which may be self-centred, lacking empathy, and focused on their own needs and desires as we've seen earlier. This stark contrast to the initial mirroring phase can be deeply confusing and emotionally distressing for the victim, as they realize they were manipulated into a false sense of connection.

Understanding mirroring in the context of narcissistic abuse is crucial for victims to recognize the patterns of manipulation and deceit employed by narcissists. By becoming aware of these tactics, individuals can protect themselves and seek support to break free from the cycle of abuse.

- **Erosion of boundaries:** Through excessive attention and charm, the narcissist aims to break down the target's defences and boundaries. This can make the target more susceptible to manipulation and less likely to question or set limits on the narcissist's behavior.

- **Emotional dependency:** Love bombing aims to create a sense of dependency within the target. By providing an intense emotional connection, the narcissist seeks to make the target reliant on their validation, love, and approval. This can make it harder for the target to recognize or leave the relationship when the narcissist's manipulative tactics surface.

- **Future manipulation:** Love bombing sets the stage for future manipulation and control. Once the target is emotionally invested and attached, the narcissist can gradually shift their behavior, withdrawing the intense affection and replacing it with manipulation, devaluation, and abuse. The stark contrast between the initial love bombing phase and the subsequent mistreatment can leave the target confused and more likely to tolerate the abusive behavior.

Narcissists devalue their victims through various tactics aimed at undermining their self-worth and exerting control. Here are some common ways narcissists devalue their victims:

- **Criticism and insults:** Narcissists frequently criticize their victims, pointing out perceived flaws, shortcomings, or mistakes. They may use derogatory language, belittling comments, or insults to demean and undermine the victim's self-esteem.

- **Gaslighting:** Gaslighting is a manipulative tactic used by narcissists to distort the victim's perception of reality. They may deny or invalidate the victim's experiences, emotions, or memories, making them question their sanity, judgment, and reality. This can lead to confusion, self-doubt, and a loss of confidence.

- **Emotional manipulation:** Narcissists are skilled manipulators who exploit the emotions of their victims to gain control. They may use guilt, manipulation, or emotional blackmail to make the victim feel responsible for their happiness or to fulfil their demands.

- **Silent treatment:** Narcissists often employ the silent treatment as a form of punishment and control. They may withdraw all communication, affection, and attention, leaving the victim feeling rejected, isolated, and desperate for their approval or attention.

- **Comparison and competition:** Narcissists frequently compare their victims unfavourably to others, highlighting their perceived shortcomings or failures. They may also create a sense of competition, putting the victim against others or against their own inflated sense of superiority.

- **Withholding love and affection**: Narcissists may withhold love, affection, or intimacy as a means of punishment or control. They may give the victim the cold shoulder or use affection as a tool to manipulate the victim into compliance.

- **Projection:** Narcissists often project their own negative traits, insecurities, or behaviors onto their victims. They may accuse the victim of being selfish, manipulative, or lacking empathy, deflecting attention away from their own actions and shifting blame onto the victim.

- **Isolation and undermining support systems:** Narcissists may isolate their victims from friends, family, or support networks. They may undermine the victim's relationships or create a dependency on the narcissist, making it harder for the victim to leave or seek support outside the abusive dynamic.

These tactics serve to break down the victim's self-esteem, create dependency on the narcissist, and maintain control over the relationship. Recognizing these behaviors and seeking support from professionals or support networks is essential for victims of narcissistic abuse.

The discard phase can be highly traumatic and emotionally devastating for the victim. The abrupt ending of the relationship or the sudden emotional withdrawal can leave the victim feeling abandoned, confused, and with significant emotional scars.

Here are some ways narcissists may discard their victims:

- **Sudden abandonment:** Narcissists may abruptly end the relationship without warning or explanation. They may simply disappear, cut off all communication, or physically leave the victim. This abandonment leaves the victim confused, hurt and often searching for answers.

- **Emotional withdrawal:** Narcissists may gradually or suddenly withdraw emotionally from the victim. They may become distant, cold, and unresponsive, showing little to no interest in the relationship or the victim's feelings. This emotional withdrawal can leave the victim feeling rejected and disconnected.

- **Devaluation and discard:** The narcissist may escalate their devaluation tactics during the final stage of the relationship. They might intensify the criticism, insults, or gaslighting, making the victim feel unworthy and unloved. This devaluation phase may culminate in a final discard, leaving the victim devastated and questioning their self-worth.

- **Idealize and devalue cycle:** Some narcissists engage in a repetitive cycle of idealization and devaluation. They alternate between periods of showering the victim with affection, attention, and validation (idealization) and then suddenly devaluing and discarding them. This cycle can create a chaotic and confusing dynamic for the victim.

- **Hoovering:** Hoovering is a term used to describe a manipulative tactic employed by narcissists to draw their victims back into a relationship or maintain control over them. It is named after the Hoover vacuum cleaner, as it signifies the narcissist's attempt to "suck" the victim back into their orbit.

Hoovering can take various forms, but the underlying goal remains the same: to regain power and control over the victim. The narcissist may engage in love-bombing, showering the victim with excessive attention, affection, and promises of change. They may apologize profusely for past behavior, expressing remorse and vowing to do better.

Alternatively, they may use guilt and manipulation, making the victim feel responsible for the narcissist's well-being or blaming them for the issues in the relationship. It is essential to understand that hoovering is not a genuine expression of change or a healthy attempt to reconcile. Instead, it is a calculated strategy aimed at regaining control and manipulating the victim's emotions. Recognizing hoovering tactics can help victims set boundaries, seek support, and prioritize their own well-being in order to break free from the cycle of narcissistic abuse.

"I am resilient, flexible, and strong. I can overcome any challenge that comes my way, and I grow stronger with each experience."
Louise Hay

Chapter Six

Narcissism Co-existing With Other Personality Disorders

Narcissistic Personality Disorder (NPD) itself is classified as a personality disorder in the Diagnostic and Statistical Manual of Mental Disorders (DSM-5). While it is considered a distinct disorder in this regard, individuals with NPD may also present with or be at an increased risk for other co-occurring or comorbid personality disorders or mental health conditions.

Some personality disorders that may commonly co-occur with narcissistic personality disorder include:

- **Borderline Personality Disorder (BPD):** There is often an overlap between NPD and BPD, and some individuals may exhibit traits of both disorders. Both disorders involve difficulties with emotional regulation, unstable self-identity, and interpersonal challenges.

- **Antisocial Personality Disorder (ASPD):** Narcissistic traits and antisocial traits can coexist in individuals. While NPD involves a preoccupation with self and a need for admiration, ASPD is characterized by a disregard for the rights of others, a lack of empathy, and a pattern of exploitative behavior.

- **Histrionic Personality Disorder (HPD):** HPD is characterized by a need for attention, excessive emotionality, and dramatic or attention-seeking behavior. Some individuals with NPD may also exhibit histrionic traits, such as a desire for constant admiration and a tendency to seek attention through dramatic means.

- **Avoidant Personality Disorder (AvPD):** AvPD is characterized by feelings of inadequacy, social anxiety, and a strong desire to avoid social interaction. Individuals with NPD may also have underlying fears of rejection or criticism, which can manifest as avoidance or social withdrawal.

However, not everyone with NPD will have co-occurring personality disorders, and the presence of comorbidities can vary among individuals. Additionally, a thorough assessment by a qualified mental health professional is necessary to diagnose and determine the specific personality disorders or mental health conditions present in an individual.

While narcissism can coexist with other personality disorders or mental health conditions, it is not necessarily the direct cause of them. However, individuals with NPD may exhibit traits or behaviors that can contribute to the development or exacerbation of other disorders. It's important to note that each personality disorder has its own unique set of causes and contributing factors.

In the next subheading we'll look at a question I get asked a lot, "what is the difference between a psychopath and a sociopath?"

My research provided some remarkable traits regarding these two disorders. However, pay close attention because although they may appear the same, a deeper understanding of personality disorders will help you recognize the distinctions between the two. I hope you find them as intriguing as I did. Please see the explanations below:

The Psychopath

A psychopath is an individual who exhibits a cluster of personality traits and behaviors associated with psychopathy, which is a specific subset of antisocial personality disorder (ASPD). Psychopathy is characterized by a distinct pattern of interpersonal, emotional, and behavioral traits. In my studies and research, I came across a teacher who introduces himself as a narcissistic psychopath all the time, but I've learnt that this is not an official diagnosis in the Diagnostic and Statistical Manual of Mental Disorders (DSM-5), but it is often used in the field of psychology and criminology to describe individuals who display specific characteristics.

Some common features of psychopathy include:

- **Lack of empathy:** Psychopaths have difficulty understanding and relating to the emotions and experiences of others. They may demonstrate a lack of remorse or guilt for their harmful actions. Although I've categorized empathy earlier, it is well to note that in the case of a psychopath, there can be more intensity to the psychopath's lack of empathy.

- **Superficial charm and manipulativeness:** Psychopaths can be highly skilled at presenting a charming and charismatic façade to manipulate and exploit others for personal gain. Whereas this is also a trait of the narcissist, psychopaths are more devious as most of their manipulations can land them in prison if they are caught.

- **Grandiose self-image:** Psychopaths have an inflated sense of self-worth and may believe they are superior to others. They may exhibit a sense of entitlement and engage in self-aggrandizing behavior. Same as the narcissist.

- **Impulsivity and irresponsibility:** Psychopaths tend to act on impulse without considering the potential consequences. They may engage in risky or antisocial behaviors without regard for the well-being of others or societal norms.

- **Lack of remorse or guilt:** Psychopaths may demonstrate a lack of remorse for their actions, even when they cause harm to others. They often rationalize their behavior or blame others for the consequences.

This is a story is to illustrate how psychopathic tendencies can play out in an individual. I'll call this guy Lucas. I share it with you as an example of how devious an individual suffering with this mental condition can be:

To those who knew Lucas, he appeared to be an ordinary and friendly neighbour. Little did they know, behind his warm smile and charismatic demeanour lurked a cold and calculating psychopath.

Lucas had always felt disconnected from the world around him. He viewed people as mere pawns in his twisted game of manipulation. His insatiable desire for power and control drove him to orchestrate elaborate schemes that left a trail of destruction in his wake.

One fateful day, Lucas set his sights on his unsuspecting neighbour, Elaine. She was a kind-hearted woman who radiated warmth and compassion. Lucas saw her as the perfect target, a challenge he couldn't resist. He meticulously studied her routines, learning every detail of her life to exploit her vulnerabilities.

Slowly but surely, Lucas began to insert himself into Elaine's life. He crafted calculated encounters, charming her with his wit and charisma. As their friendship grew, Lucas gained her trust, making himself indispensable to her.

Unbeknownst to Elaine, Lucas was manipulating her every move. He planted seeds of doubt and fed her insecurities, gradually isolating her from her loved ones. With each passing day, Elaine became more dependent on Lucas, completely unaware of the web he was weaving around her.

Lucas's true nature started to reveal itself when Elaine stumbled upon a shocking discovery. She stumbled upon a hidden room in Lucas's basement, filled with newspaper clippings detailing past crimes and unspeakable acts of violence. It became clear that Lucas was not the person he pretended to be.

Terrified and desperate to escape, Elaine devised a plan to expose Lucas's true nature to the world. She gathered evidence and reached out to the authorities, determined to bring him to justice. But Lucas, always one step ahead, anticipated her move and launched a counterattack.

In a tense and harrowing showdown, Lucas revealed his sinister side. He held Elaine captive, revelling in her fear and vulnerability. However, he underestimated Elaine's resilience and inner strength. In a moment of courage, she fought back, using her wit and resourcefulness to outsmart him.

With the authorities closing in, Lucas's facade finally crumbled. He was apprehended, and the truth about his psychopathic nature came to light. The community was left shocked and disturbed, realizing how easily evil was hidden behind the mask of normalcy.

Elaine, though scarred and isolated from her loved ones, managed to emerge as a survivor. She returned to her family telling them of her ordeal and asked for their forgiveness for her distancing and lack of communication, while she lived a life of fear with Lucas.

It was a challenge for her, but she eventually found solace in the support of her loved ones, and the strength she had discovered within herself. As for Lucas, he was sentenced to a lifetime behind bars, separated from society.

The story of Lucas serves as a chilling reminder that evil can exist even in the most unsuspecting individuals. It reminds us to remain vigilant and to trust our instincts, for sometimes "the most dangerous monsters are the ones that walk among us unnoticed."

Psychopathy is a complex and controversial concept, and the term should be used with caution.

Only trained mental health professionals can provide a proper diagnosis based on comprehensive assessment and evaluation.

N.B The stories shared are for illustrative purposes only. Any semblance of actual stories is purely coincidental.

The Sociopath

A sociopath, also known as antisocial personality disorder (ASPD), is a psychological condition characterized by a persistent pattern of disregard for the rights and feelings of others. Individuals with sociopathy often exhibit manipulative, deceitful and impulsive behaviors.

They do so without feeling remorse or empathy for their actions. Here are some key features associated with sociopathy:

- **Lack of empathy:** Sociopaths have difficulty understanding or experiencing empathy for others. They disregard the feelings, needs, and well-being of those around them.

- **Manipulative tendencies:** Sociopaths are skilled at manipulating others to achieve their own goals. They may use charm, deceit, or coercion to exploit and control people in their lives.

- **Deceptive behavior:** Sociopaths frequently engage in lying, dishonesty, and deceit as a means to manipulate others or to achieve personal gain.

- **Impulsivity and irresponsibility:** They often exhibit impulsive behavior, acting without considering the consequences. This can lead to a disregard for societal norms, rules, and obligations.

- **Lack of remorse or guilt:** Sociopaths do not feel genuine remorse or guilt for their actions, even when they harm or manipulate others. They may rationalize or justify their behavior to avoid taking responsibility.

- **Shallow emotional range:** Sociopaths may have a superficial or shallow emotional range, showing little genuine emotion or displaying emotions that are primarily self-serving.

- **Chronic violation of social norms:** Sociopaths consistently disregard and violate societal norms and rules, often engaging in illegal or immoral activities.

Here's an illustrative story about Alex and Sarah to help you understand further how sociopaths behave.

Alex, a charming and charismatic individual, seemed to effortlessly win over everyone he encountered. He had a captivating smile and a magnetic personality and always presented himself as a caring and trustworthy friend. However, beneath the surface of his charm and charisma, Alex had a dark secret that no one in his circle was aware of.

One day, Alex's co-worker, Sarah, shared her dreams of starting her own business. Intrigued by the potential opportunities, Alex quickly befriended Sarah, offering his support and guidance. He gained her trust, promising to help her achieve her goals and navigate the challenging world of entrepreneurship.

As time passed, Alex quietly began to manipulate and exploit Sarah's vulnerabilities for his gain. He skilfully stole her business ideas, and presented them as his own, while he sabotaged her opportunities behind the scenes. Sarah, unaware of Alex's true intentions, trusted him completely and felt grateful for his guidance.

But as the deceit unfolded, Sarah started to notice inconsistencies and discrepancies. She confronted Alex, hoping for an explanation, only to be met with deflection and gaslighting. Alex effortlessly shifted blame onto others and twisted the truth, making Sarah doubt her own perceptions and sanity. The emotional distress caused by Alex's actions left Sarah feeling utterly betrayed and confused.

Despite the disbelief, betrayal and hurt inflicted on Sarah, Alex remained calm and composed, expertly masking his true intentions from those around him. Sociopaths, like Alex, have an uncanny ability to adapt their personalities to fit any situation. They use their charm and charisma as powerful tools to manipulate and exploit others for their benefit.

It is important to note that sociopathy is a complex condition, and not all individuals with Antisocial Personality Disorder (ASPD) will exhibit the same traits or display them in the same way. Each case is unique, and a diagnosis of sociopathy should only be made by a qualified mental health professional based on a comprehensive evaluation of an individual's behavior and symptoms.

Recognizable Traits of Sociopathy from Alex's Story:

- Superficial charm and charisma
- Manipulation and exploitation of others
- Lack of empathy and remorse for their actions
- Ability to deceive and lie convincingly
- Grandiose sense of self-importance
- Shallow emotions and a tendency towards impulsivity
- Lack of regard for societal norms and rules
- Tendency to engage in risky or antisocial behavior
- Inability to form genuine emotional connections
- Skilful adaptation of their personality to fit different situations and manipulate others.

It is crucial to approach the topic of sociopathy with care and seek professional guidance when dealing with individuals who may exhibit these traits.

NB. The stories shared in this book are for illustrative purposes only. Any semblance of actual stories is purely coincidental.

"We may be unique, yet our journeys often echo shared stories. In life's twists, there's a silver lining waiting to be discovered. Embrace the search for positivity, for it's in seeking the good that we truly thrive."

Sue Barker

Chapter Seven

(Test Yourself)
Identify Narcissistic Traits in the following Stories

Rachel's story

Rachel was a bright and ambitious young woman in her mid-20s. She was independent, and caring, and had a genuine desire to make a positive impact in the world. Her kindness and empathetic nature made her vulnerable to the manipulative tactics of a narcissistic partner.

Rachel met Mark at a social gathering. He was charming, charismatic, and seemed genuinely interested in her. Mark showered Rachel with attention, compliments, and affection, making her feel special and loved. Over time, however, Rachel began to notice subtle signs of control and manipulation.

Mark gradually isolated Rachel from her friends and family, portraying them as a negative influence in her life. He convinced her that he was the only one who truly understood her and that their relationship was superior to any other connection she had. Rachel started to distance herself from her loved ones, believing that Mark's love was enough.

As the relationship progressed, Mark's behavior became increasingly demanding and critical. He would constantly belittle Rachel's achievements, dismiss her ideas, and undermine her self-confidence. He would claim that he knew what was best for her and that she couldn't trust her judgment.

Whenever Rachel attempted to assert herself or express her needs, Mark would swiftly turn the situation around, making her feel guilty for having those desires. He would twist her words, manipulate her emotions, and gaslight her into believing that she was overreacting or being unreasonable.

Rachel's self-esteem plummeted under the weight of constant criticism and invalidation. She became increasingly dependent on Mark for validation and approval, desperately seeking his love and acceptance. She felt trapped and powerless, unable to escape the toxic cycle of emotional abuse.

Eventually, Rachel reached a breaking point. One morning she heard me while I was featured on a local radio station and decided to call me after the show. Rachel confided in me and I immediately recognized the signs of narcissistic abuse and encouraged her to learn more.

With the awareness she got from my research and other members, she was eventually able to understand that Mark needed help and that she could not fix him. After months of trials backwards and forward with Mark, she began to accept what she was now learning about narcissism and how it relates to what she was experiencing.

Rachel learned about narcissistic abuse, the tactics used by manipulators, and how to establish healthy boundaries. She slowly rebuilt her support network, reconnecting with loved ones who had been pushed away. With time, Rachel regained her confidence and embraced her inner strength to reclaim her sense of self-worth and independence.

Leaving the toxic relationship was not easy, as Mark continued to manipulate and harass her, but Rachel was determined to break free from his control. She obtained a restraining order and surrounded herself with women from our TTNAWH foundation where she is a member of a strong support team.

Rachel's journey of healing was challenging, but she emerged from the experience with newfound resilience and self-awareness. She became an advocate for survivors of narcissistic abuse, using her own story to raise awareness, support others, and empower them to break free from the cycle of abuse.

In Rachel's story, several narcissistic traits and tactics can be identified. Were you able to identify the following traits?

- **Love-bombing:** Mark initially showered Rachel with excessive attention, compliments, and affection to quickly establish a strong emotional bond and make her feel special.

- **Isolation:** Mark gradually isolated Rachel from her friends and family, portraying them as negative influences, to control her and ensure she was solely dependent on him for support and validation.

- **Belittling and criticism:** Mark consistently undermined Rachel's self-esteem by belittling her achievements, dismissing her ideas, and criticizing her, eroding her confidence and making her doubt herself.

- **Manipulation and gaslighting:** Mark manipulated Rachel's emotions, twisted her words, and made her question her own reality. Gaslighting is evident when he convinced her that her reactions were overreactions or unreasonable.

- **Control and power:** Mark exerted control over Rachel by asserting that he knew what was best for her, diminishing her ability to make decisions or trust her own judgment.

- **Hoovering:** Despite the toxicity and abuse, Mark continued to harass and manipulate Rachel even after she tried to break free, attempting to draw her back into the relationship.

It is important to recognize these narcissistic traits and tactics to better understand the dynamics of the abusive relationship and provide support to survivors like Rachel.

N.B The stories shared in this book are for illustrative purposes only. Any semblance to actual stories is purely coincidental.

Sharmila's Flight

Sharmila was only 15 when her father decided to marry her off to his best friend, Elton. Her father, Ram, a struggling farmer, believed that it would be best for his eldest daughter to start a new life. Elton assured Ram that he would take care of Sharmila. However, things quickly took a turn for the worse.

Soon after their marriage, Sharmila gave birth to a baby boy, but Elton's affection began to fade away. He started mistreating her in unimaginable ways and warned her not to tell her father about it. Elton developed a habit of coming home drunk after hanging out with his friends, and Sharmila lived in constant fear of him. As soon as he arrived, he would physically abuse her for the slightest thing.

This cycle of abuse continued for many years, and Sharmila found no relief. Eventually, she reached out to someone overseas who contacted me to share her story. Sharmila wanted to escape from Elton but was terrified to stay in Trinidad. She desperately sought a way out for herself and her son, hoping to find safety abroad.

When I spoke to Sharmila, she revealed that she hadn't eaten in four days. This was her punishment for not having Elton's meal ready on time when he came home. She lived in constant terror of him, so she followed his rules and refrained from eating, despite still having to cook for him and their son.

Shamla reaches out to social media where her plight was heard and she was eventually rescued from the clutches of her abuser. Not all stories of escaping narcissistic abuse are as severe as Shamila's case. Sometimes cognitive therapy can rescue both victim and perpetrator. It depends on the severity of the case. Sometimes persons can be referred to the relevant authorities who will provide the necessary resources to bring relief.

In this story of Sharmila, it appears both her father and her husband possessed narcissistic traits. Here are some traits that can be recognized in both characters from this illustration:

- **Lack of empathy:** Ram disregards Sharmila's well-being and imposes his decision to marry her off to his best friend without considering her wishes or feelings.

- **Objectification:** Ram treats Sharmila as a means to solve his own problems (financial struggles) by arranging a marriage for her without considering her happiness or consent.

- **Lack of accountability:** Ram fails to take responsibility for the consequences of his actions, such as the abusive situation Sharmila finds herself in after the marriage.

- **Emotional and physical abuse:** Elton engages in consistent mistreatment and physical abuse toward Sharmila, demonstrating a lack of empathy and control over his anger.

- **Power and control:** Elton exerts power and control over Sharmila through physical abuse, intimidation, and creating an environment of fear.

- **Substance abuse:** Elton's habit of coming home drunk and engaging in abusive behavior suggests a lack of self-control and disregard for the well-being of his family.

These individuals exhibit traits commonly associated with narcissism, such as a lack of empathy, a need for control, and a disregard for the feelings and well-being of others. It is important to note that a proper diagnosis of narcissistic personality disorder would require a comprehensive assessment by a qualified mental health professional.

In Sharmila's case, it was crucial for her to escape the abusive environment and seek help to break free from the cycle of abuse. The support provided by organizations like TTNAWH can be instrumental in assisting victims like Sharmila in finding safety, healing, and rebuilding their lives.

N.B The stories shared in this book are for illustrative purposes only. Any semblance to actual stories is purely coincidental

Chapter Eight

The Repercussions of Narcissistic Abuse

Being in a relationship with a narcissistic individual can have significant consequences for one's physical health due to the chronic stress and emotional turmoil endured. The relentless cycle of emotional abuse, manipulation, and psychological distress takes a toll on both the mind and body. Here are some common physical illnesses that can be affected by the stress of narcissistic abuse.

Firstly, the constant state of stress and anxiety experienced in a narcissistic relationship can contribute to chronic fatigue. The emotional strain and psychological exhaustion can disrupt sleep patterns, leading to persistent feelings of tiredness, low energy levels, and a general lack of motivation.

The digestive system is also vulnerable to the effects of stress. The body's stress response can interfere with normal digestion, leading to digestive problems such as irritable bowel syndrome (IBS), stomach ulcers, acid reflux, or gastrointestinal discomfort. The connection between emotional stress and digestive health is well-documented, and the ongoing stress in a narcissistic relationship can exacerbate these issues.

Another area of impact is the immune system. Prolonged exposure to stress weakens the immune system's ability to function optimally, making individuals more susceptible to infections, viruses, and other illnesses. The constant state of anxiety and emotional distress associated with narcissistic abuse can compromise the immune system's ability to defend against pathogens, leading to a higher likelihood of falling ill.

Headaches and migraines are also common physical symptoms associated with the stress of narcissistic abuse. The heightened tension and emotional strain experienced in such relationships can trigger frequent headaches or migraines. The physiological response to stress, including muscle tension and constriction of blood vessels, can contribute to the development or exacerbation of these conditions.

Furthermore, chronic stress has been linked to cardiovascular issues. The prolonged activation of the body's stress response can lead to high blood pressure, increased heart rate, and inflammation, which can eventually contribute to the development of heart disease or other cardiovascular problems.

It's important to recognize the impact of narcissistic abuse on physical health and take steps to prioritize self-care, seek support, and implement stress-management techniques. Consulting with healthcare professionals, therapists, or support groups specializing in trauma recovery can provide valuable guidance and assistance in addressing both the emotional and physical consequences of narcissistic abuse.

Victims of narcissistic abuse can also experience a range of psychological, emotional, and interpersonal effects as a result of their interactions with narcissistic individuals. Here are some common characteristics or effects experienced by victims of narcissistic abuse:

- **Low self-esteem:** Narcissistic abusers often undermine their victims' self-worth and self-confidence. Constant criticism, gaslighting, and manipulation can lead to a diminished sense of self-esteem and self-belief.

- **Emotional instability:** Victims of narcissistic abuse may experience heightened emotional reactivity, mood swings, anxiety, depression, or feelings of emptiness. The abusive tactics employed by narcissists can create a state of emotional turmoil and instability.

- **Self-doubt:** Due to the consistent invalidation and manipulation, victims may develop a persistent sense of self-doubt. They may question their own judgment, perception, and abilities, constantly seeking external validation.

- **Guilt and self-blame:** Narcissistic abusers often shift blame onto their victims, making them feel responsible for the abusive behaviors or situations. Victims may internalize this blame, leading to feelings of guilt, shame, and a distorted sense of responsibility.

- **Isolation:** Narcissistic abusers often isolate their victims from friends, family, and support systems. They may create a dependency on themselves and undermine the victim's social connections, leaving them feeling isolated and alone.

- **Hypervigilance:** Victims of narcissistic abuse may develop a state of constant alertness and hypervigilance to the abuser's moods, reactions, and demands. They may anticipate and try to prevent conflicts or negative outcomes, always walking on eggshells.

- **Boundary issues:** The manipulative tactics of narcissistic abusers often blur boundaries and violate personal space. Victims may struggle with setting and maintaining healthy boundaries in relationships, leading to difficulties in asserting their needs and protecting themselves.

- **Trust issues:** The betrayal, deceit, and emotional manipulation experienced in narcissistic abuse can erode a victim's trust in others. They may find it challenging to trust their own judgment and may approach new relationships with caution and scepticism.

- **Post-Traumatic Stress Symptoms:** In severe cases of narcissistic abuse, victims may develop symptoms of post-traumatic stress disorder (PTSD). Flashbacks, intrusive thoughts, hyperarousal, and avoidance behaviors can be triggered by memories of the abuse or reminders of the abuser.

Breaking free from the chains of narcissistic abuse requires immense strength and support, with therapeutic healing and a focus on rebuilding one's sense of self-worth and boundaries as essential steps towards reclaiming a life of empowerment and resilience.

What type of Individuals do Narcissists target?

Narcissists tend to target individuals whom they perceive as vulnerable or easily manipulated. While there is no specific "type" of person who is always targeted by narcissists, certain characteristics or circumstances may make individuals more susceptible to becoming victims of narcissistic abuse. Here are some factors that can make someone a target for narcissists:

- **Empathetic and compassionate individuals:** Narcissists are drawn to individuals who are empathetic, caring, and willing to prioritize others' needs. They exploit these qualities for their own benefit and may take advantage of the victim's willingness to give and nurture.

- **Low self-esteem or insecurity**: Individuals who have low self-esteem or struggle with feelings of insecurity may be more susceptible to the manipulation and gaslighting tactics of narcissists. The narcissist may prey on their vulnerabilities, offering false validation and using it as a means of control.

- **People-pleasers and caretakers:** Those who have a strong desire to please others or tend to prioritize the needs of others above their own are often targeted by narcissists. Their selfless nature can be exploited by the narcissist, who takes advantage of their willingness to accommodate and satisfy their demands.

- **Co-dependent individuals:** Narcissists often seek out individuals who have a tendency toward co-dependency. Co-dependent individuals may have an excessive need for validation, struggle with boundaries, and have an intense fear of abandonment, which the narcissist can exploit and manipulate to maintain control in the relationship.

- **Trusting and forgiving personalities:** People who are inherently trusting and forgiving may be more likely to give the narcissist multiple chances and believe in their promises to change. Narcissists often take advantage of this willingness to forgive by repeating patterns of abusive behavior.

- **Individuals experiencing life transitions or vulnerabilities:** Narcissists may target individuals who are going through challenging life transitions such as divorce, bereavement, job loss, retirement or other significant changes. During vulnerable

SUE BARKER

times, victims may be more susceptible to manipulation and may seek support or validation from the narcissist.

Women should pay close attention to their perimenopause and menopause onset as this is a significant transitional period in a woman's life. It brings about hormonal changes that can impact various aspects of physical, emotional, and mental well-being. Narcissists, who are skilled at exploiting vulnerabilities, may perceive menopause as an opportunity to further manipulate and control their victims.

They may capitalize on the emotional and physical challenges women face during this phase to further their agenda. By seeking out emotional "fuel," which refers to the attention, admiration, and reactions they crave, narcissists can exploit the vulnerable state of menopausal women. The emotional roller coaster often associated with menopause, coupled with the narcissist's manipulative tactics, can leave women feeling even more overwhelmed, confused, and emotionally drained.

The narcissist may use these vulnerabilities to assert power and control over their victims, exacerbating their emotional distress and perpetuating the cycle of abuse. By understanding the dynamics of narcissistic abuse and taking steps to prioritize their own well-being, menopausal women can empower themselves and work towards healing and regaining control over their lives.

Men who experience andropause also build up insecurities in mid-life, especially if they are experiencing narcissistic abuse. They may find themselves trapped in a tumultuous emotional state. The constant manipulation, gaslighting, and criticism from the abuser can severely damage their self-esteem and self-worth. As they navigate the challenges of mid-life changes and confront their mortality, the emotional impact of the abuse can be intensified.

They may feel a profound sense of confusion, isolation, and vulnerability, as their abuser systematically undermines their confidence and distorts their perception of reality. The emotional toll can lead to anxiety, depression, anger, and a deep longing for validation and a sense of purpose. Breaking free from the grip of narcissistic abuse and rebuilding their emotional well-being requires support, therapy, and a commitment to self-discovery and healing.

In essence, narcissistic abuse can have significant effects on both women and men experiencing mid-life changes. While the impact can vary depending on individual circumstances, here are some general ways narcissistic abuse can affect individuals during these stages of life:

- **Emotional well-being:** Narcissistic abuse often involves manipulation, gaslighting, and constant criticism, which can severely damage a person's self-esteem and emotional well-being. During mid-life changes, hormonal changes, and aging, individuals may already be more susceptible to feelings of vulnerability, and narcissistic abuse can exacerbate these emotions.

- **Self-image and body image:** Mid-life changes and aging can bring about shifts in one's physical appearance and self-image. Narcissistic abusers may exploit these insecurities, making derogatory comments about their partner's appearance or using age-related insults to demean them. This can lead to a distorted body image and a deepening sense of inadequacy.

- **Isolation and loneliness:** Narcissistic abusers often isolate their victims from friends, family, and support networks. During mid-life changes and aging, individuals may already be experiencing shifts in their social circles due to various life transitions. The combination of narcissistic abuse and these changes can lead to increased isolation and feelings of loneliness.

- **Health and well-being:** Hormonal changes and aging can bring about physical and mental health challenges. Narcissistic abuse can further exacerbate these issues by causing chronic stress, anxiety, and depression. It may also lead to neglect of one's health as the focus becomes survival within the abusive dynamic.

- **Identity crisis:** Mid-life changes, hormonal fluctuations, and the process of aging often prompt individuals to reflect on their life choices, goals, and sense of self. Narcissistic abuse can distort a person's perception of their own identity, leaving them feeling lost, confused, and disconnected from their authentic self.

- **Financial dependence:** Narcissistic abusers often exert control over their victims by creating financial dependence. During mid-life changes and aging, individuals may already be facing financial challenges related to retirement planning or career transitions. The added burden of financial control within an abusive relationship can further undermine their sense of security and independence.

- **Resistance to change**: Individuals experiencing mid-life changes, hormonal fluctuations, and aging may be more resistant to change and less willing to confront the abuse they are experiencing. This resistance can stem from fear of further destabilizing their already tumultuous life circumstances or a sense of hopelessness that change is even possible.

The effects of narcissistic abuse can be long-lasting, and recovery may require professional help, support from loved ones, and a commitment to self-care and healing.

Remember that anyone, regardless of their personality traits or circumstances, can become a victim of narcissistic abuse. Narcissists are skilled manipulators and can target a wide range of individuals. Recognizing red flags, setting and maintaining boundaries, and seeking support are important steps in protecting oneself from narcissistic abuse.

The Empath

The empath is an individual who possesses a heightened sensitivity to the emotions, needs, and experiences of others. They have a deep capacity for empathy and compassion, often feeling and absorbing the emotions of those around them. Here are some key points to understand about empaths:

- **Emotional Sensitivity:** Empaths are highly attuned to the emotions of others. They can easily pick up on subtle cues and energies, often experiencing and feeling emotions as if they were their own. This sensitivity allows them to deeply connect with others and offer support and understanding.

- **Compassionate Nature:** Empaths genuinely care about the well-being of others and have a natural inclination to help and support them. They often prioritize the needs of others over their own, making them nurturing and selfless individuals. Their compassionate nature makes them excellent listeners and sources of comfort for those going through difficult times.

- **Absorbing Others' Emotions:** Empaths have a tendency to absorb the emotions of those around them, which can be both a blessing and a challenge. While this enables them to connect deeply with others, it can also lead to emotional exhaustion and overwhelm if they do not have healthy boundaries and self-care practices in place.

- **Intuitive Abilities:** Many empaths possess strong intuitive abilities, allowing them to sense and understand things beyond what is explicitly communicated. They can often pick up on unspoken cues, hidden emotions, and underlying dynamics in relationships or situations.

- **Healing and Helping Roles:** Empaths are often drawn to healing and helping professions, as their innate empathy and understanding make them well-suited for roles such as counselling, therapy, nursing, or social work. They have a natural ability to provide comfort, guidance, and support to those in need.

- **Idealistic and romantic mindset:** Individuals who have a romanticized view of relationships and love may be attracted to narcissists, as they can initially appear to embody the qualities of an ideal partner. Their charm, confidence, and grandiosity can be captivating to those seeking a passionate and intense connection.

Empaths need to practice self-care and establish boundaries to protect their emotional well-being. They should learn to differentiate between their own emotions and those they absorb from others, as well as develop strategies to manage and release any emotional burdens they may carry.

In relationships, empaths may need to be mindful of their tendency to prioritize others' needs over their own. They need to establish healthy boundaries and communicate their own needs and limits to maintain balance and prevent burnout.

Overall, empaths play a valuable role in society by offering empathy, understanding, and healing to those around them. By embracing their gifts while also taking care of their emotional well-being, empaths can positively impact the lives of others and contribute to creating a more compassionate and empathetic world.

An Empath's Story

Here's a typical example of an Empath's journey:

Tammy, an empathetic individual, is in a relationship with Dante, who exhibits narcissistic tendencies. Dante recognizes Tammy's caring and empathetic nature and uses it to his advantage.

In the beginning stages of their relationship, Dante showers Tammy with excessive affection, compliments, and attention. He makes her feel special and desired, appealing to her empathetic nature. This tactic, known as love-bombing, creates a strong emotional bond and makes Tammy feel valued.

As the relationship progresses, Dante starts to manipulate Tammy's emotions. He uses guilt, shame, and emotional blackmail to control her behavior and get what he wants. Whenever Tammy expresses her own needs or disagrees with Dante, he gets defensive and accuses her of not caring about his feelings or being selfish.

Dante consistently undermines Tammy's perception of reality through gaslighting. He distorts the truth, denies his actions or behaviors, and makes Tammy doubts her memory or judgment. For instance, when Tammy confronted Dante about an incident where he was disrespectful, he twisted the events, accused her of being crazy and overly sensitive. He then shifted the blame onto her.

Dante takes advantage of Tammy's empathetic nature by making her responsible for his emotional well-being. He constantly demands her attention, support, and validation while showing little regard for her own needs.

He manipulates her into sacrificing her time, resources, and energy for his benefit, often leaving Tammy feeling drained and depleted. To maintain control of her, Dante attempts to isolate Tammy from her support network. He discourages her from spending time with friends and family, undermines her relationships, and portrays himself as her sole source of love and validation.

This isolation makes Tammy more dependent on him and less likely to seek help or escape the toxic dynamic. Over time, Dante devalues Tammy's worth and contributions, eroding her self-esteem and confidence. He belittled her accomplishments, criticized her appearance, or constantly compares her unfavourably to others.

The outcome of this is inevitable as history has proven in situations such as this. Eventually, when Dante feels he has gained sufficient control, he may discard her without warning or explanation. This will inevitably leave Tammy confused, hurt, and questioning her worth.

This is a typical example of how a narcissist exploits an empath's empathetic qualities for their benefit, often resulting in emotional manipulation and a cycle of psychological, emotional and even physical abuse in some cases. This cycle will continue until the victim either rises to the occasion to rescue themselves through knowledge and support or until either one passes away.

Initially, Dante uses love-bombing to win Tammy over, showering her with excessive affection, compliments, and attention, tapping into her desire for love and validation. However, as the relationship progresses, Dante's true intentions become clear.

Dante manipulates Tammy's emotions by using guilt, shame, and emotional blackmail to control her behavior and fulfill his own needs. He disregards her own needs and opinions, accusing her of not caring about his feelings or being selfish whenever she expresses herself.

Through gaslighting, Dante distorts the truth, denies his actions, and undermines Tammy's perception of reality, leaving her feeling confused and questioning her judgment.

Exploiting Tammy's empathetic nature, Dante makes her responsible for his emotional well-being, demanding her constant attention, support, and validation while showing little regard for her own needs. He isolates her from her support network, discourages her from spending time with friends and family, and portrays himself as the sole source of love and validation in her life.

Dante devalues Tammy, belittling her accomplishments, criticizing her appearance, and comparing her unfavourably to others, causing her self-esteem to diminish.

In this toxic dynamic, Tammy finds herself drained and depleted, questioning her own worth and feeling trapped in the relationship.

It is important for individuals like Tammy to recognize the manipulative tactics and seek support to break free from such exploitative relationships, focusing on their own well-being and rebuilding their self-esteem.

N.B The stories shared in this book are for illustrative purposes only. Any semblance of actual stories is purely coincidental.

The Super Empath

The term "super empath" is often used to describe individuals who possess even higher levels of sensitivity, empathy, and intuition than the average empath. Super empaths have an extraordinary ability to understand and connect with others on a deep emotional level. Here are some key characteristics and traits associated with super empaths:

- **Heightened Sensitivity:** Super empaths have an incredibly heightened sensitivity to the emotions and energies around them. They can pick up on subtle cues, vibrations, and shifts in the emotional atmosphere. This sensitivity allows them to perceive and understand the needs and experiences of others with exceptional accuracy.

- **Deep Empathy:** Super empaths have an innate ability to empathize deeply with others. They can step into someone else's shoes and experience the emotions and perspectives of others as if they were their own. This profound empathy enables them to provide immense support, compassion, and understanding to those in need.

- **Enhanced Intuition:** Super empaths often possess heightened intuition and psychic abilities. They have a strong sense of inner knowing and can trust their instincts and gut feelings to navigate various situations. This intuition helps them sense the underlying truth, motives, and dynamics in relationships and interactions.

- **Emotional Resilience:** Despite their heightened sensitivity, super empaths often exhibit emotional resilience. They have a strong capacity to endure and process intense emotions, both their own and those they absorb from others. They can bounce back from challenging situations and continue to offer support and care to others.

- **Boundary Setting and Self-Care:** Super empaths recognize the importance of setting healthy boundaries to protect their own emotional well-being. They understand that self-care is essential to recharge and replenish their energy reserves. They engage in practices such as meditation, journaling, nature walks, or creative outlets to maintain balance and prevent emotional burnout.

- **Healing and Transformative Presence:** Super empaths have a transformative presence that can positively impact the lives of others. Their ability to deeply understand and connect with people allows them to facilitate healing, growth, and positive change in others. They often inspire and uplift those around them through their authentic presence and empathic abilities.

While being a super empath can be a gift, it's important for individuals to be mindful of their own needs and practice self-care. They should be aware of their boundaries, learn techniques to differentiate their own emotions from others and prioritize their own well-being to prevent emotional exhaustion.

Super empaths have the potential to make a profound difference in the world by spreading empathy, understanding, and healing. Their ability to connect deeply with others and facilitate positive change can contribute to creating a more compassionate and empathetic society. I often say that a super empath is a narcissist's worst nightmare.

N.B The stories shared are for illustrative purposes only. Any semblance to actual stories is purely coincidental.

What Determines a Narcissist or an Empath growing up under the same Conditions?

The development of personality traits, including whether a child becomes a narcissist or an empath, is a complex interplay between genetic factors, individual temperament, and environmental influences. While growing up in a toxic environment can contribute to the risk of developing narcissistic traits, it doesn't guarantee that every child exposed to such an environment will become a narcissist.

Children who receive emotional validation, empathy, and support from their caregivers are more likely to develop empathy themselves. If a child's emotional needs are consistently met, they are more likely to develop prosocial and empathic traits.

The quality of early attachments formed with primary caregivers can shape a child's sense of self-worth and its ability to relate to others. Secure attachment promotes a healthy neurological process, while insecure or disorganized attachments may contribute to the development of narcissistic or empathic traits.

Other environmental factors such as peer relationships, school environment, cultural influences, and societal values can also impact a child's development. These factors can either reinforce narcissistic tendencies or promote empathy and healthy social interactions.

While these factors can contribute to the development of narcissistic or empathic traits, they do not provide an absolute prediction. Each child's journey is unique, and individuals can exhibit a wide range of behaviors and traits influenced by various factors. Hence the reason why it is crucial for primary care givers to provide a well-balanced healthy life style, and be a very prominent part of their children's lives.

"Gratitude turns what we have into enough, and sharing our stories turns our lessons into treasures that enrich the lives of others."
Sue Barker

Chapter Nine
My story

Cycles One

Damien was charming, very attractive or "pleasing to the eyes" as he described himself. He wasn't too tall, had a flat stomach, and you can see that he took great care of himself. He did this for more than one reason, which you'll learn about later. He was well-known in his profession, and he achieved high-ranking status over the years making him well-respected by his subordinates.

Although he was now in his fifties, he really looked great and I admired that about him. He was my schoolmate and friend for many years so it was easy to have a conversation with him because we had a history that went back many years.

I hadn't seen him for quite a while though, but that day was their sports and family day so there he was with his handsome self, looking all fit and familiar. My sister and I were invited by someone else, so when I saw him, I was surprised because I thought he was already retired. He was also surprised to see us and greeted us with a warm embrace.

As a Senior Officer, he had his own table, after chatting for a few minutes he invited us to share his table. He immediately called his subordinates to attend to us. We were served with food and drinks in abundance. I had to tell him that I was driving and to hold up on the drinks. We laughed about it and enjoyed his company for a couple of hours. At the end of the day, we exchanged numbers and went our separate ways.

After reaching home that night I got a call from Damien checking to ensure I got home safely. That was thoughtful of him because he knew I had had a few alcoholic drinks. We spoke for a while expressing how nice it was to see each other again and planned to do it again sometime.

He invited me whenever I'm in the area to give him a call and we can probably do lunch or something. I agreed saying, "I'll be looking forward to that."

A couple weeks after that night, I was working in that area so I called to let him know I'll be on that side. He seemed happy to hear that and said he would have them prepare a place for me at the head table so I can have lunch with him. His rank allowed him that privilege.

That sounded great and your girl was feeling special. I got there around twelve thirty and everything was set. He met and escorted me to the dining area where I was met by his subordinates and was escorted to my seat at the table.

We had a lovely lunch and after we were finished eating, he invited me to the lounge area where we sat on two leather sofas facing each other while sipping on some Jack Daniel's and coconut water. We spoke for hours about our kids, our careers, our mistakes, our relationships. We spoke about my parents whom he knew, (they are both deceased now). Damien told me that he recently buried his mother.

I was a bit surprised to hear that he had buried her because, I can't remember him ever having a close relationship with his mother. I remembered him mentioning that his father had passed away when he was very young at some point during school days. He was just a year and a half old when it happened, so he barely remembers him, except from pictures. He grew up with his aunts and uncles and some brothers and sisters that he visited from time to time.

Since I knew Damien, he never spoke much about his father until now. He told me that his father was a bodybuilder and he had several women. He learned this when he got older and was told that after his father passed away, he was left with his stepmother to care for him. He was the last of about fifteen children for his father and they were scattered all over because there were at least eight different women who were their mothers.

Over the years he lived with several of his relatives because his step-mother was working. She also passed away soon after his father, making Damien's life a little more unstable. I felt really sorry for him at this point and all I could think about was how I could make him understand that it was not his fault.

The things he shared with me made me feel closer to him for some strange reason. By the time the evening was over, Damien had made a great impact on me. His revelations about his family background and his tumultuous upbringing evoked feelings of empathy and compassion within me.

Understanding the challenges he faced, and the instability he experienced throughout his life made me want to provide support and reassurance that everything was going to be ok. I just wanted to fix it for him.

I left there thinking, "How was it that we never gotten close?" Despite some of the challenges he spoke about with past relationships he had matured quite nicely". After all, "don't we all have some skeletons in the closet?" I thought to myself as I began warming up to the idea of sharing more of these moments with him.

He was suave! He looked great in his uniform, and he was clean and handsome. He had a flat stomach, (oh, did I already mention that he had a flat stomach…. lol) bandy legs, brown complexion, and a great sense of humour. Damn he smelled good. "This is trouble," I thought to myself.

While driving home the thoughts about certain things we discussed played back in my head. Some of which I smiled at and some made me cringe. I chose to fantasize about the ones that made me smile.

Throwing all caution to the wind. I began to fantasize about how good we could be together, if only we gave it a chance. I was not considering my own well-being, neither was I thinking about such boring things as trust, respect, boundaries or anything of the sort. Those qualities would only interrupt the flow of what was in the future for Damien and me.

I knew my capabilities and I believed I could make him happy. It seemed so easy to do, and then we would live happily ever after! Right? There were so many red flags from that conversation, but I was unaware at that time. I just saw what I wanted and believed in my heart that if given the chance I could make a difference.

It would be just what we both needed, I could fix things and then he would not have to be the way he was in those other relationships. This would be different. I was very optimistic about that.

It's understandable that when we have strong feelings for someone, we may be inclined to overlook or downplay certain red flags.

We might believe that we have the power to change or fix the person, hoping for a different outcome compared to their past relationships. This optimism and desire for a positive connection are not uncommon.

However, it's important to approach these situations with a balanced perspective. While it's natural to want the best for someone and believe in the potential for growth and change, it's crucial to recognize that people's behaviors and patterns are deeply ingrained and often difficult to alter solely through the efforts of another person.

Over the next couple of weeks, Damien kept in touch via text messages, "a whole lot of them." It was a little eerie at first, but I managed to convince myself that it was because we were special to each other. Then, one day he casually invited me to his home for Sunday lunch. He said "his wife" (yes, he was married), "was out of the country. But she had filed for a divorce before she left.

He went on to explain that "she would be back soon, in time for the Court proceedings." He was sure that after this he was going to be a free man. "That wasn't such a bad status," I thought, after all I knew him first, right? lol.

The situation with Damien was becoming more complicated but I was not interpreting it that way. I was blinded by the fact that we had been through enough and we had now found each other. We both had the desire to be together and that it was now our time to make and keep each other happy and contented with life.

At least if we decided to get into relationship, he will not be a married man at that time. That was my "Note to self."

My response to Damien's invitation was, "Let me sleep on it, I would let you know early enough so you can prepare just in case if I decide to come." He said, "Okay. But I'm really hoping you say yes". I smiled to myself but I did not respond.

I thought about it throughout the night, "should I, should I, should I?" After much deliberation I decided I would go. I knew that he could not make me do anything I did not want to do, but that was not the issue.

The thing that bothered me the most was that he was married and this is the house he called home with his wife. But that little devil with the fork standing on my shoulder kept telling me "Go, you'll be ok. You know you can handle it."

To be honest, I really wished his situation were different, because deep in my heart I wanted to go. I felt we deserved to find out what or if we missed anything from our youth. He called around ten o'clock the following morning to see what I decided. I told him I would come, but I was going to finish cook at my home first. He sounded excited when I answered him and I found it a bit amusing.

I was experiencing some very conflicting emotions in this situation. On one hand, I had a desire to explore a potential connection and see what we may have missed in our earlier years. On the other hand, I was fully aware of the complexities and potential ethical concerns associated with getting involved with someone who is still married. But you see, in my mind, Damien was different. He was "my Damien" from school! My first attraction as a teenager and I somehow felt entitled to explore what we had missed.

The following day, I took a fruit bag with me and a bottle of non-alcoholic grape wine. When I arrived at his home, he could not conceal his excitement. I wore a black and white lounge dress and my hair was in a simple bun. He looked at me from head to toe and said, "you look nice", I said "thank you". That calmed the awkward moment. He wore sweat pants and a T-shirt over his slender body, which he maintained well over the years, he looked nice, clean, and simple.

As Damien invited me inside, I could not help but feel that I was assisting him in crossing some boundaries here at his home. Although I knew it was wrong, I felt a bit entitled because it was Damien! A little voice was telling me that this should have been my life, he should have been my husband but the other voice was shouting, "snap out of it".

The reality was that it was uncomfortable being in another woman's space but, I was also observing how comfortable he was entertaining me there. Why was it that I had all this confusion brewing in my mind but I could not stop myself?

I wondered to myself, "was this a normal thing for him to entertain women at his home when his wife is away?" Then the Devil with the fork on my shoulder answered and said, "No, you are special to him, remember how long you've known each other." I liked that thought so I began to get a little bit relaxed at that moment.

I asked if he needed help with anything to which he replied, "No I'm done here". He poured me a drink, while I sat at the table to eat. The meal was excellent. He made a biscuit pie, which I never had before, callaloo, baked chicken, red beans, mixed rice and green salad. It was impressive. We had lovely conversation during and after the meal.

When we were finished, he served dessert, which he boasts of making himself. It was coconut ice cream and upside-down pineapple cake. It was divine! While I was having dessert, Damien brought out four photo albums. He opened them up one by one, page by page, and he proceeded to share the history of each photo. I must admit at first, I was impressed at how proud he was of his family.

He began with his five children and all their achievements over the years. There were photos of himself in his various uniforms throughout the thirty something odd years. They were a hell of a lot, and as if that was not enough, he began pointing out all the trophies, badges, and pins that he had at home from his years in the military. He did not fail to mention that, that was only part of his collection, the rest were at his office.

As Damien showcased his life's journey, I began to wonder at a certain time, of his reason for doing so in such detail. While it was interesting at the beginning, it soon began to get monotonous.

I was trying to keep an optimistic view that he really wanted me to understand his journey in the event that we decided to get serious at giving "us" a chance at love. But was it that Damien thought he needed to do this as a reflection of his personality or did he have a need for validation?

What I did not know at that time was that this was a means of asserting his status or to prove to me how important and accomplished he was.

He offered me a drink of Jack Daniels which I welcomed because it was needed after that two-hour long lesson of his family history.

The evening was turning out to be somewhat relaxing, that is once I had dismissed the possible red flags that were before me. Instead, I began to imagine what it would be like to be in a relationship with him. Other than his obsession with his achievements and all the different photos of himself at different stages in his life, he was really cool.

I convinced myself of that. At this time, I was invited to a tour of the three-bedroom house he called home. He showed me everything including the master bedroom which was now labelled the "wife's room," then of course came his room. I guess he wanted to prove that they weren't sleeping together and that the marriage was really over. I believed him because in my mind he had no reason to lie to me.

Or was it that I was already being suckered in? He was very patient, not in a hurry at all. As I reflect on that time, with the knowledge I now have, I see that every move was well calculated like a hunter preparing the trap for his prey. He observed me closely as I began to fall for his bait, while I was not in the least bit suspecting of Damien's underlying schemes.

I knew of his wife for many years, they always had a very unstable relationship resulting in him fathering five children with three different women. She also knew of me as "Damien's friend from school", but we never really had a conversation per say. I respected her for who she was to him over the years. She was the mother of two of his daughters for several years.

There was a separation during those years and she migrated, got married to someone else that she stayed married to for nine years and somehow, they both ended up back together and married! From what he explained, it was more a marriage of convenience that the traditional love story.

Now the complexities of Damien's relationships should have raised some concerns, not so? But this was "my Damien" from school. I believed that I could fix whatever was broken in his life, once we had that chance. We reminisced about our lives. The good, the bad and the in-betweens. We discussed my parents, who are now deceased.

He surely reminded me of how fond they were of him. He was correct indeed. I believe my father admired Damien in his uniform because he reminded him of himself as a young man when he also served in the Army.

As for my mother, I would say this, parents long ago always believed that a man in uniform was respectable, financially secured and would make a good husband for their daughter. To top it off Damien was good-looking and very mannerly. Mammy adored him and wanted him to be her son-in-law. She even voiced her sentiments over the years.

Although several years had passed, Damien never gave up on visiting them while they were alive. Even long after, I had moved out of the family home and was on my own, he kept in touch with everyone in my family. I lived at several locations over the years and I swear he visited me at all of them at some point. Another reason why I trusted him so easily, I truly believed we had something special.

As the conversation continued, I asked what he did for fun and he replied, "Sometimes I meet people, sometimes I go to the casino, I spend a lot of time at work and when "Madam" travels I'm home mostly". "Meet people you say?" was my response. He replied with a shrugged shoulder and said, "Well you know I am not getting any sex at home, right?" I then replied, "Ok, I understand".

I thought I did. I was looking at that statement from regular point of view, however, now that I know better, I look back and I understand that someone with NPD cannot survive without narcissistic fuel. Whenever they are running low on fuel, they will seek supply from any secondary source. The person who would pay them a compliment no matter how insignificant we may think it is, it will work as fuel for the narcissist. So, at the grocery store, the gas station, the car wash, the church or even folks that they have not seen for a long time would suffice. Wherever they can get that emotional response, they will show up, ready to feed.

Looking back at it he received a secondary source of fuel from us over the years. Because I used to be genuinely happy to see Damien and so was my family over the years whenever he popped up. And then he would disappear for months or even years. But he would always show up at some point.

Overall, I thought the date went well except for the part when he tried to make a pass at me in his wife's room, he casually invited me to "come watch a movie in here", as he gestured to the room. That invitation was uncomfortable, but again I dismissed it as him trying to reach out to me because of his feelings toward me after all these years. It was forty-one years since I knew Damien at that time, so I did not think he wanted to get me in an uncompromising position.

Honestly, I am not even sure I knew what to think at that time. I refused to see Damien as the type that would stoop that low to try to seduce me, especially on a practical first date. Remember this is someone I trusted and felt we had a safe friendship. Nonetheless, I did not give in to his little gesture. Instead, I just laughed it off, as I found it quite amusing at our age. He was noticeably shaking which I found was even more amusing.

I must admit that I felt a different connection between us when I left there that evening. I began to dream of what it would be like if I were to give "us" a chance. I had never experienced that with him before. "This is crazy", I kept thinking to myself, "After almost forty-one-years girl?" At this time in my life, I was single so the timing to give this a shot was perfect.

After all we are mature people now, we've been through the dramas of life and relationships and pretty much knew what we wanted and most of all, what we didn't want at this stage of our lives.

The anticipation of a possible chance at "true love" was exciting, only because of who I believed Damien was to me. Anyhow, after that special evening we began dating regularly. We would meet up during the day at different locations for lunch, we went to the movies, and we spent hours on the phone texting and talking all during the day and all night.

We began exercising together and I was happier than I'd been in years. I looked forward to his messages. At times he sent me R and B oldies with quotes and matching emoji of love expressions which I thought was so cute. This actually made me feel like a teenager again and I loved it. I didn't think it was possible to ever feel that way again.

Nothing else mattered at this point, except what I was envisioning with Damien. The stage was being set for the perfect relationship the one that I always dreamt of. Little did I know I was now entering the love bombing stage of a relationship that would change my life in ways that was beyond my imagination!

I was sure that we were well suited for each other and that I would spend the rest of my life with him. He was the blast from my past, "this was our time, and "it is going to be perfect" I thought to myself. He was happy! Even his friends said things to me that assured me that I was making a positive difference in his life since we began seeing each other.

He certainly appeared fuller of life when we were together now, than when we had just started dating.

He even said that I made him happy, and he feels so complete with me. I was very convinced that I had made the right choice to give "us" a chance. Although we were not together for a long time we had history, we had life experiences and a strong desire to be together.

That was more than enough to commit to making this work. Everyone loved Damien and found we were a perfect match. We really looked great together, if I may say so myself. He is a couple of inches taller and we are about the same complexion and size. The man had a flat stomach, (I guess by now you would realize how important that is to me, right?), and was toned in all the right places from being a physical Instructor and trainer for the Special Forces in the Army. He was fitter than a fiddle and he was as grandiose about it as can be.

What I didn't know is that this was a huge red flag because as I learnt subsequently, narcissists are instinctively charming. They can literally charm the pants off most of their preys. Their first impression is usually a lasting one. This charm is a necessary tool for them to keep a supply handy because they must never run short.

Making Damien "happy" at this time was effortless, and seeing him like this made me happy. An unbelievably emotional experience that did not compare to anything I had ever experienced in my younger years. Because of our history and the intensity of our desires to be with each other, it only took a little over two weeks before we became inseparable. We were perfect together. A type of "perfect" that felt unreal at times.

I just could not understand why I was getting the feeling that this was "too good to be true". Nevertheless, I shook off that negative energy any time it presented itself because nothing was spoiling this for me. I would justify it by making comparisons to past relationships and again, "who Damien was to me." I had been lied to, cheated on and taken for granted in relationships prior to this, but I was convinced that this was going to be different.

It was a different time, a different individual, everything about this was different and we have a history of attraction for each other that never got to develop into an intimate relationship until now! This was our time to make this right. So, I kept dismissing those negative thoughts each and every time.

On another note, Damien had a great sense of humour, a bit corny at times, but he managed to make me laugh a lot, sometimes at the joke and sometimes at how stale the joke was. Overall, he made me laugh, and to me, that was a positive thing. By now I was convinced that Damien was not only my soul mate he was my physical mate also. We fit well together which made intimacy with him a magical experience. When we were together like this nothing mattered. The world didn't seem to exist. It was like floating around in space amongst the stars. "This was it," I thought to myself on every occasion. I had finally found the one whose rib I had from creation.

Nothing could ruin this for us because he shared the same sentiments, or so I thought. I believed that everything I felt he was feeling it too! He would look me in the eye while we made love and ask, "Why you never gave me the opportunity before?" I stared back at him, not knowing what to say. It was as if he took the thoughts right out of my head. "You should have been the mother of my children." I laughed and said "no sir, I am quite happy with who my children are."

Anyways, he seemed just as happy and satisfied as I was and it was perfect. We spoke about travelling together to visit his kids. We spoke about him getting his divorce finalized, we even fantasied about getting married one day in Tobago on the beach barefooted in the sands. Damien became everything I ever hoped for in a partner, and I made sure to let him know how much I loved every moment of being with him.

I felt safe! So why not? Right? He cooked, cleaned, and took great care of his home. He had potential. I remember saying to him, "I could put you in house, man," and both laughed it off. Damien loved to shop at the department store in the city. He even shopped for personal items for me, this drew me even closer to him. I felt like he was really taking care of me, just the same way he took great care of himself and smelt so fresh and clean all the time.

It was truly amazing to be having that experience at this time of my life. I surrendered my mind, body and soul to what we had now found in each other, it was unbelievable!

Cycle Two

I thought we were both on the same page, until one day after just five weeks of floating on a cloud Damien's mood began to change without reason. There were moments when I would sense the tension in him. It was as though he was deliberately angry with me for no reason. He just lay stiff on the bed as if he was restricted to that one spot, his face expressionless. This made me very uncomfortable and confused.

Whenever I asked why he was being like that, he got defensive. He would say things like "You don't know what I'm going through, I am dealing with a lot right now. At times he would accuse me of nagging him when I was just trying to understand what he was going through so I could try to help him, in whatever way I could. Sometimes he would mention briefly that it's either a situation from work, or "home", which is how he referred to his wife any time he had to speak about her.

Damien indirectly led me to believe that the main reason he was like that was due to the pending divorce, and that he did not want to lose his home. He had worked hard to acquire it he was still paying a mortgage. So, to have to battle for it in a divorce was not something he was looking forward to. I believed him and I was willing to give him that moral support during the process. I used to say to him, "Babe, you have to keep a positive mind-set and you will see how things will work out in your favour soon." Sometimes he just looked at me with emptiness in his eyes.

The "golden phase" or "the new relationship energy" was truly amazing, it appeared as if that was exactly what Damien wanted as well. Unfortunately, I later found out that that was an instinctive reaction and I was taking the bait hook line and sinker into his web.

Naturally, when you are attracted to someone, and you are receiving positive energy from that individual, the hormones begin to do their own thing. This causes an overload of Endorphins, Dopamine, Oxytocin, and Adrenaline etc. All the feel-good hormones were present, and the prime aim was being achieved every step of the way. This is what creates that addictive emotional entanglement.

I later found out that his peers called him "the beast" because of the duration of his exercise routine each time he worked out. Damien is known for working out for hours in the blazing sun completing many different routines. He did this at least three times weekly to keep in shape. I eventually understood why this was a necessary tool for him in the scheme of things.

I admired Damien's prowess routines and didn't think anything negative of it at the time, but engaging in rigorous exercises at least three times weekly can be influenced by narcissistic traits for a few reasons. Firstly, narcissistic individuals often crave admiration and validation from others. They may view their physical appearance as a key aspect of their self-worth and believe that rigorous exercise will help them maintain an attractive and admired image, ultimately seeking praise and attention from others. Damien often tried to challenge his colleagues, but no one was willing to go up against him.

Secondly, individuals with narcissistic traits tend to have a strong desire for control and superiority. Regular exercise allows them to exert control over their bodies, adhere to strict routines, and exhibit discipline. He often spoke about his physical ability comparing himself with those that were younger than he was, and their inability to challenge him. When I learnt that persons with these traits may perceive their physical fitness and prowess as a way to assert their superiority over others and reinforce their belief in their own exceptionalism, I was convinced that I was on to some answers regarding what I was experiencing with Damien.

Cycle three

About six weeks into the magic, I began to experience something different. The magic was dwindling slowly, becoming normal or let's just say not as intense as it was. At first, I was not too concerned, although it was like experiencing slight turbulence, you know the kind that startles you and then it settles? Yes, that kind. I figured we would pick up again when the altitude is regularized, so at first, I was not too concerned. But Damien began playing with his phone a little more than usual.

The attention to his phone gradually increased over the coming days. His text messages to me when he was at work began to decrease, even the content of the messages began changing, from, "I miss you so much." "I can't wait to see you later", "wish we had done this several years ago", "I never enjoyed anyone as much as I enjoy being with you", "I wish you were the mother of my children" and so on, to "I'm not sure if you'll see me later", "I had a long day in work", "I can't speak right now", "I'll call you back", The slightest question I asked was met with, "Why are you accusing me?" or if I wanted to see him, his favourite line was, "We'll see how it goes".

Oh, how I have learnt! Looking back, I can see now that when the objective is achieved the interest begins to shift into the next phase of the cycle. All of the attention and seemingly happy times was only about achieving the prime aim, that ultimate "control." Saying "I love you" to him was like the switch that turned the cycle on.

He accomplished his goal, I was now in his web, his matrix of persons that he places on the shelf for the next rounds. I was clueless so the narcissistic cycle continued. So, what happened next?

Damien's wife was due back to Trinidad in a few days' time and his behavior toward me was getting increasingly distant. He began going to the Casino where he spent several hours at a time trying to take his mind off of the "impending Court matter" he said. He went into this sudden depression that created knots in my stomach.

I interpreted it as him being uncomfortable to face the repercussions of the divorce. But we had spoken about this at length, "so what was the problem?" I asked. The answer he gave was that he "did not know what to expect". He was concerned about his home and what he would do if he loses something that he worked so hard for. I accepted his explanation as genuine at first, maybe because I wanted it to be true. But intuition was doing a number on me.

Damien's frequent visits to the casino started to evoke memories of my father's own gambling addiction, which had a significant impact on my life as a child. This realization was unnerving, and my concerns deepened as I noticed the increasing duration of time Damien spent there.

Subsequent to this experience with Damien, as I delved into the study of narcissism, I realized that individuals with this disorder often struggle with addictions, ranging from drugs and alcohol to sex and even gambling. This newfound understanding prompted me to reexamine my experiences with Damien through this lens of addiction and narcissism.

In my next book, you will gain further insight into the profound influence of my father, and the intriguing connection between the triggers of Damien's gambling addiction.

As Damien continued with his explanations, they began to sound like a broken record, he gave me the same explanation over and over with just a little twist of least conviction each time. By this time, I was already ensnared, I just didn't know it. I saw big, old, fat lies in front of my face and refused to believe that is what was happening.

I wanted it to be what I wanted and, I was not settling for less. In the situation all I could have done was offer my confused support and hope that the knots in my stomach would soon fade away.

As the days passed, I was becoming more and more anxious and I began to question my-self. "Did I make a mistake letting this man into my life? I began to feel guilty wondering if there is some possibility that he's considering rekindling the marriage. But, "how could this be after we spent such quality time together?" I asked myself these questions over and over again but only came up with more questions, no answers. I began to retrieve emotionally trying to prepare myself for any disappointment that would present itself with this new and unexpected turn of events.

But no matter how I tried I could not find a comfortable space within to rest my conscience and concerns for me to be at peace with it.

I was now convinced that I was in love with Damien, and it was very hard to turn back. It had to be love right? What else could make you feel as though your whole world would crumble without this individual? I couldn't understand it, but apparently those feel-good hormones were doing some numbers on my whole self along with my intuition.

During those six weeks, yes would you believe that it was just six weeks and I could not turn off the desire for more of what Damien and I shared? I wanted that rush, that feeling that only he could satisfy. Not just the sex, but all that he was to me during that time. In some foolish way he became the centre of my world and he knew it.

The day came and Damien went to pick up his wife at the Airport. I was in a hot mess. I didn't know how to feel or what to expect. But to my surprise he dropped her home and, he came straight to me. When this happened, I began to see things differently and fell for the entrapment even more. I began opening up to him again, surrendering my-self, mind, body and soul even more. I was now convinced that nothing could separate us.

It seemed that all his concerns were put to rest on her arrival because he was in a different mood. I had no idea what they spoke about and I did not want to know. My only concern was that he was in my arms, wanting me and showing me that I was all that mattered.

We spoke at length that night and he admitted that he was not sure how he was going to handle the divorce. I assured him again, that no matter the outcome that I would be there for him. Her reason for being back, he said, was to go through with the divorce. His main concern was the house that he did not want to lose. I felt that I needed to be gentle on him.

I really began to believe that he was having a midlife crisis and needed a great deal of support. So, I made up my mind that night to stand beside him, after all, isn't that what love supposed to do? After spending the night at my home, Damien left the following morning for work. It was not long after he called to tell me that his engine had caught on fire and that he was awaiting some assistance from his workmates.

This happened about twenty minutes away from the Base where he was headed. He stayed in touch during the day keeping me updated as to what was the situation with the vehicle. I assured him that if he needed my help in any way that I would be happy to help, but he said he's ok, but if he does, he would let me know.

That evening Damien messaged me to let me know that he would be staying on the Base. He said he got in touch with the mechanic but the guy would not be able to visit him until the following day to sort out the problem with the vehicle. In the past Damien spent a lot of nights on the Base, sometimes working overnight or sometimes when he was just too tired to drive out or up to mischief I realized after.

So anyways, I was not on to his façade at yet, so when he told me he was staying down there I was fine with it, it seemed the logical thing to do.

Damien spent the next couple of days tending to the vehicle, (or so I thought). He had to get an engine and this was posing a bit of a challenge according to him. Nonetheless, on the third day after the incident he visited me with a different car which he explained he borrowed from a friend. I thought nothing of it at that time. He spent the night at my home and left the following morning to go see about purchasing the engine for his car.

But OMG…..!!!! "Why did intuition have me so uneasy?" The little time we'd been together there was no one that he spoke about that he had that closeness with, enough to borrow their vehicle. He would have rather rented one based on the personality he painted for me. I tried to dismiss it, but it was like a boomerang, the thoughts kept coming back at me so hard that it became more difficult to do so.

The following day he came to my home with the same car and by then I was sure my intuition was going to come through my mouth. I tried to be cool about it, but I had to ask, "Babe who is your friend that owns this vehicle?" he watched me as if to say, "How dare you ask me that?" He shook his head, as if he was in disbelief of my question.

He continued unpacking stuff from the car and taking it inside. I then said, "I'm serious, who's car, is it? He then looked at me and said "it belongs to a friend, her name is Ms. Patsy, ok?" I responded with raised eyebrows, "Ms. Patsy?" to which he did not reply. His mood changed from trying to convince me that there was nothing more to it, to being so angry that he was raising his voice at me in a matter of seconds.

Something I never saw coming. I was really taken aback to the point where I could not even react. You know I had to find out more about this "friend" whose name is Ms. Patsy, right? So, we had the talk. He said that he had a relationship with Ms. Patsy for three years but it was over. "It was over?" I asked. To which he responded, "yes, it is a situation that should have never happened", he said with what I interpreted to be disgust in his voice.

He went on to explain that Ms. Patsy was a young lady that was younger that his last daughter. He met her at some games that were held at the Stadium and she was very helpful at the event where he ran in the hundred meters dash. She was there to give him and others water and rags etc. They got into conversation and one thing led to the next and they began dating. He said he knew it was wrong but things at home weren't so good and he found her to be a refreshing alternative.

It bothered me that he could be with someone younger that his daughter, it bothered me that he hadn't told me about this before we got so involved. It bothered me that she would have admired him and maybe even loved him enough to lend him her car and for so long. I had so many questions at this time, but I tried to keep it inside and not pry too much. It didn't help. I prepared dinner but couldn't eat.

The questions filled me up. My chest was hurting with the need for clarity regarding this new development. He didn't engage me with answers. Instead, he got angrier with each attempt I made to understand what I had gotten myself into.

Eventually I tried to leave it alone, but it was at the forefront of my mind until I asked him to leave. I told him I couldn't do this. "It is too early in the relationship for this type of hurt", I said to him. He didn't say another word, he just left. I don't know which was worst, the fact that he didn't offer further explanation or the fact that he didn't seem to be bothered that I asked him to leave.

I did not hear from Damien for two days. This was digging a dark hole in the pit of my stomach as my emotions went into overdrive. I imagined all sorts of things like him being there with her, making love to her if he was enjoying her as much or maybe more that he enjoyed being with me. I felt used. I wished the earth could open and take me in. I was embarrassed! But most of all I began to judge myself for allowing him with his whole married self to entice me into this situation. I couldn't pray because I felt dirty.

God knew that I know better, therefore I began trying to hide from Him in my pain.

There was no one I could turn to for comfort or to get answers. I was broken and felt like a fool. How could "my Damien," whom I had grown to love so deeply betray our love like this? I tried calling him on the third night, he did not answer at first and I tried again, and again. He answered on the third try. It was amazing how unbothered Damien sounded! I was furious and at a loss for words, all that escaped me was, "where are you?"

He answered in a very jovial tone, "I'm up by this girl here, I may spend the night because my car wasn't ready yet and the garage is close to where she lives". I could not believe my fucking ears, "really", I screamed. "You gotta be fucking kidding me," I said with tears in my eyes, disbelief in my mind and a dagger through my heart and soul.

There were a lot of chatter in the background and I instantly wondered if the joke was on me. I knew he heard the tears in my voice, but he just did not acknowledge it. I told him he needs to come see me now because I am not handling this too well. It was the worst emotional experience I've ever had, "what the fuck is wrong with me?" I kept asking myself, but there were no answers forthcoming at this time. What went wrong? Things were moving along so smoothly. I was in utter disbelief. In answer to my request he said, "I don't understand why you are sounding like that but okay, I'm on my way."

I couldn't sit still. I paced up and down while crying my heart out for all of the twenty-five minutes it took, for him to reach my home. When Damien arrived, he came out of the car, yes, the same car as if nothing happened. He began a totally different conversation about some incident at work and how he handled it. I sat there looking at him in disbelief and wondering if I was going crazy. I couldn't say anything for at least fifteen minutes.

When I did find my composure, I looked at him and asked in the most concerned voice, "what the fuck is wrong with you Damien?". He looked at me as though he was in shock at the question, "what you mean?" he asked. He went on to say, "you asked me to come and I came, what's the problem now?".

By this time, I needed a drink, something strong or a smoke in something because my head was just about ready to pop open, I swear. I remembered when we were in school Damien always seemed different. He was always very neat, always packing his school bag with something, either his books, his football clothes, his scout gears or something.

At that time, I thought he was very organized which is not a quality you find in young school boys around that age. He was admired for his neatness, the way he dressed and his hair. He had a big afro which was the trending hairstyle at that time.

Something about that guy was just different. Even in the years when we went our separate ways from school and had our families and so on, anytime I happened to see him, the question would always be at the back of my mind, "what is it about Damien that is so different"? It wasn't a different bad, nor was it a different good, it was just a mysterious different that I couldn't put my finger on.

As a financial consultant, I am well aware of the constant opportunities for growth and development in my line of work. However, amidst the tumultuous state of my love life, I found it incredibly challenging to focus on anything else besides the ongoing saga with Damien.

Questions plagued my mind, and I couldn't help but ask myself, as well as him, "what was truly happening here?" In one conversation, Damien had the audacity to tell me to relax and explained that he was working on extricating himself from the situation with the young lady he had been involved with. He claimed that she looked up to him as a father figure and had even threatened to take her own life if he were to leave abruptly. According to him, he was trying to handle the situation delicately out of kindness.

I couldn't believe what I was hearing. Did this man not realize the extent to which he had pursued me, reeling me in completely? It was as if he had no clue about the emotional rollercoaster, he had put me through, mind, body, and soul, I muttered to myself, "what the fuck did I really get myself into with this mad man?"

At that point, my emotions were completely shattered. I found myself visiting him at his workplace, spending hours immersed in discussions about his situation with Ms. Patsy, his divorce, and contemplating what our future together could hold. Despite my gut feeling that he had been dishonest about many things, I desperately wanted those lies to be true. So, I listened, I cried, and I professed my love to him. This pattern continued for two weeks until I finally gathered the courage to end the triangulation with Damien, Ms. Patsy and myself.

I did not understand that what I was experiencing was the triangulation phase of a narcissistic relationship until long after. Therefore, this situation I found myself in with Damien only evoked a multitude of intense emotions within me. I was confused, hurt, and emotionally drained.

Initially, I was in shock, then I felt betrayed, and I began to question myself and him. "Is it that I am not good enough? What more do you desire Damien?" I was on a rollercoaster with fits of rage, jealousy, sadness and insecurities. I wanted to talk to her, to find out what….I really didn't know! But I needed answers.

This is exactly what the triangulation phase does to you, it can leave the victim feeling trapped, isolated, and emotionally exhausted, as they struggle to navigate the complex web of emotions and the dynamics of the narcissistic relationship.

Over time, this phase can erode the person's self-esteem and confidence, leaving them emotionally vulnerable and questioning their own worth. It often becomes a pivotal point where they begin to recognize the toxic nature of the relationship and may find the strength to seek support, regain their independence, and ultimately break free from the cycle of narcissistic abuse. But it was not time yet.

Cycle Four

For nearly five months, I hadn't spoken to Damien. I assumed that he had reconciled with Ms. Patsy and that they were now together again. Slowly but surely, I began to regain control over myself. It was an arduous process, but the most challenging part was behind me. I came to the realization that I didn't want to be entangled in the chaotic mess that Damien had created in his life, and I was ready to move forward.

During my time apart from Damien, I decided to focus on my studies, and it proved to be a positive turning point for me. Although I was hurt and disappointed, I realized that I would be okay. While it didn't turn out to be the fairy tale I had hoped for, I was grateful that I was able to end things relatively early.

Despite the short duration of our relationship, the feelings I developed for him were unlike anything I had ever experienced before. There were moments when I deeply missed him as if a part of my soul had been taken when he left.

I confided in my sister and friends, discussing the negative emotions he had caused me. It wasn't about involving others in my personal affairs, but rather an attempt to free myself from those thoughts that weighed on my mind. Gradually, I regained my composure, although I still couldn't completely remove him from my thoughts. It was perplexing to me.

One morning, while I was on my way to the city for work, minding my own business, I found myself stuck in traffic. To my surprise, guess who was right beside me? It was Damien, driving in the same direction, presumably heading to work as well. In a moment of impulsiveness, I honked my horn, feeling a mix of anxiety and anticipation in the pit of my stomach that was now reserved for anything related to Damien. In response, he signalled for me to pull over, and he did the same. I parked my car behind his, and we both stepped out.

He asked if I had already had breakfast, and I replied with a no. Gesturing towards a nearby breakfast shed that overlooked the sea, he suggested we go there. It was a popular spot where they served local breakfast, and we could enjoy the serene view of the water and passing boats. The scenery was breathtaking. We ordered coconut bake and fried fish along with two drinks and sat down together, to savour the meal.

All this time very few words were spoken. While we began eating, he asked how I was doing. I said "I'm doing okay" (with shrugged shoulders). "You?" I asked, to which he replied, "I'm okay." We both ate our breakfasts hardly saying anything to each other, just being there. As for me, I may not have been saying anything out loud but the knots in my stomach had resurfaced as if they were just waiting for the signal.

My inside was literally in shambles and my hormones were just out of control. I felt sorry for me, and I wanted to kill him. I also wanted to squeeze the truth out of him until he was blue in the face, but I don't think I would do well in prison. I swallowed everything I was feeling and said nothing about nothing!

When we were through Damien motioned to hug me and I unwillingly gave in to it, while I thanked him for breakfast. He then surprised me with the question, "What time would you be home?" Normal old me would have dealt with that question in a whole different way, but disappointed, hurt and delusional me, just said, "around five". He just said, "okay, I'll check you later." He was smooth, I didn't know how else to respond and I was not happy I was that vulnerable.

As the day progressed, I could not control the anxiety that seemed to be on steroids whenever Damien was around. The truth is, I was longing for Damien to hold me, I wanted him to tell me that everything I was thinking was not true and that he'd been home trying to get his life together. But deep down I knew that was not true.

Some part of me was willing to accept that he was not going to leave this young lady. But the other part that, figuratively shows up on my shoulder with the pitch fork, led me to believe that she was as vulnerable as he was making her out to be. I think Damien wanted to believe that she really needed him.

It made me sick to my stomach but somewhere in my mind I still believed I could fix this and we can be happy together eventually. Why was I determined to make this right? Why with all the red flags that I was seeing I was not able to resist Damien? I did not have the answers, and it was eating at my soul. I could not say no to him when he visited me that evening.

He came in his usual fashion as if he never stopped. He brought four cases of water, bread and some other drinks that he brought into the kitchen and said to me, "put this away" while he handed me an envelope with some money. By this time, I was at a loss for words which was becoming a regular occurrence with this man now. "Who is this man? What sort of sick game is he playing with me?" I took the envelope and placed it on the dining table. I asked if he was hungry to which he replied, "yes, but not for food" in his usual corny way trying to make humour.

In retrospect, I came to realize that my bond with Damien was rooted in the trauma he had been putting me through. At the time, I was blind to his true nature and only saw the false self he had initially presented. It was this idealized version of him that I yearned for, not the cold and unfeeling person he ultimately revealed himself to be eventually.

We sat at the dinner table to have a sandwich that I prepared and he began to tell me about situations at work with some of his colleagues. He spoke about his situation at home with his wife and the divorce proceedings. They were receiving mediation from the family court in an effort to salvage the marriage. "Really?" I said to him in disbelief. "After all you've told me about the breakdown of your marriage you are now going to mediation?" I couldn't believe my ears. I felt like a hamster on a wheel!

As I reflect on this journey, I recognize one of the common characteristics of narcissistic personality disorder (NPD) or narcissistic traits in Damien's behavior at that time. You see the narcissist is capable of hoovering or drawing a person back into a relationship with them, while picking up right where they left off as if no time had elapsed.

The same blame game, conversations, arguments everything replays itself as if the relationship was never interrupted. This was uncanny, it felt so unreal because I didn't understand it at the time.

Damien dismissed my question while he proceeded to call his friend on the phone asking him in a joking manner, "you will never guess where I am?" I did not hear what his friend said but he responded by telling him where he was. He continued to have a conversation with the guy on the phone for several minutes while ignoring my questions completely. After almost an hour of that distraction, he began complaining about being tired and yawning. I knew he wanted to stay.

The absurd thing is that I, in some sick, twisted, helpless way also wanted him to stay.

I was still hopeful although Damien wasn't saying what I wanted to hear, I still yearned for him to hold me and make it all go away. All the pain, confusion and anxiety I thought I had buried before seeing him that day, all surfaced again. I did not have the strength to put them back to rest. "Why?"

When Damien came off the phone, he asked me if it was ok if he spent the night because he was too tired to drive home. Pretending not to be too enthusiastic about the idea I answered and said, "you can stay, but you'll have to stay in the spare room". He said "okay mam", he then went to get his overnight bag out of his vehicle. Damien did not go to the spare room.

He boldly took his bag directly to my room. I did not have the emotional strength to resist him. He spent the night, the elephant remained in the room and we were back at it as if nothing happened.

Damien began staying at my house regularly over the next three to four weeks. Things seemed a bit normal for a while, he began flooding my phone with text messages once again and phone calls. Damien would call to tell me he was going to have lunch.

Then he called to tell me what he had for lunch. Anything he was doing he checked in with me. It was very overwhelming, but I figured that he just wanted me to feel comfortable that he was not playing any more games. He slept over regularly during this time and things were going great.

During that period, Damien got invited to two events, both on the same night. A boat ride and his friend's birthday party. He said we'd go to the boat ride first and then we'd go to his friend's birthday party. The boat ride was finishing early so it was do-able. I must admit that I was really happy at that time with Damien and slowly began to let down my guard once again. I really thought we were making some progress with our relationship this time around.

We wore white that night, him in a white shirt and jeans and me in a white fitted jump suit, looking all sophisticated and sexy, if I may say so myself. We looked good together. The music was great, the people were well dressed and the whole atmosphere was conducive to having a great time. Damien dances well and I love that about him. I love to dance so things were absolutely perfect as far as I was concerned.

That was until Damien suddenly decided to leave me standing there without a word and went to do a head count, it seemed. At first, I thought he went to the bathroom, but after twenty minutes had passed, I began to feel uncomfortable. I knew he could not have left me there because we were out at sea, but he could have at least said something! He showed up about twenty-five minutes after with no explanation. Naturally, this generated a subtle tension between us, or so I felt.

When the boat ride was over, we left to head to the birthday party. I tried really hard to pretend that his actions did not bother me. We were now on our way to his friend's house. I was hoping to break the tension so we could continue enjoying the evening, things had started off so lovely. However, things did not go according to my expectations.

When we arrived at the party, Damien left me standing in a corner and went to interact with his female friends without even introducing me. Instead, he went on engaging in extensive conversations with these four women. This distressing scene went on for at least forty-five minutes! I was so embarrassed until I eventually told him I was ready to leave.

What I learnt in my analysis, subsequent to my studies, was that by deliberately leaving me there isolated and disregarding my feelings, Damien was able to assert dominance and superiority. This power dynamic reinforced his perceived sense of entitlement and this made me feel vulnerable and inferior.

Moreover, it was a form of manipulation and gaslighting, as his actions undermined my self-esteem and created a sense of insecurity in a very subtle manner. This emotional manipulation further solidified how much Damien was controlling me without me realizing what was happening. He was able to gain fuel without effort, because I was furious, and he loved it.

We got home around three thirty in the morning and that's when I decided I needed to find out what the hell that was all about. I explained to Damien how I found his conduct was very embarrassing and inappropriate. He seemed astonished and failed to acknowledge any wrongdoing saying that I was making an issue out of nothing. He basically said I was over reacting! Trying to explain to Damien what he did and how it made me feel was an absolute waste of time.

The conversation went around in circles, as I tried to explain to Damien how his actions affected me. I could not understand how he was not getting the points I was trying to make. As I continued to explain how hurt and embarrassed I felt. He nonchalantly changed the topic to something about seeing Mr. Smith when we were on the boat.

Damien went on to explain that he had a conversation with Mr. Smith and that that is the guy from the store he was telling me about. The one with the son that wanted to get in the Army. He continues explaining who Mr. Smith was and how many children Mr. Smith had etc. I swore I was in a movie with this man, because I had no idea what I was dealing with at the time.

Narcissists often engage in what is known as "word salad" and circular conversations, which can have profound effects on their victims. Word salad refers to their tendency to use confusing, nonsensical, or manipulative language, making it difficult for the victim to follow or make sense of their statements. This intentional obfuscation serves to maintain control and create chaos, leaving the victim feeling disoriented, frustrated, and doubting their own sanity.

Circular conversations, on the other hand, involve the narcissist repeatedly deflecting, evading, and changing the subject, preventing any meaningful resolution or addressing of concerns.

This tactic leaves the victim feeling unheard, invalidated, and trapped in a never-ending cycle of confusion and emotional exhaustion. Over time, these communication patterns erode the victim's self-esteem, undermine their confidence, and can lead to a sense of powerlessness and self-doubt.

Now that I look back on this time with Damien it is clear, that what I was experiencing was all that is mentioned in the forgoing paragraph. A significant point to note is that Damien behaved on instinct. When he was faced with a situation that he could not provide answers for, his narcissism would take over to protect him. It would then cause him to behave in the appropriate manner to protect himself from the shame, guilt, stress or whatever was necessary at the time.

As I looked in the direction of the window, I saw the sun was coming up and Damien and I were still at it. I was determined to get some clarity on his behavior, it was mind boggling. I just could not leave it alone. Adding to the complexity of the situation, Damien suddenly began crying, I mean really crying tears as if someone had died! I was so startled! I tried to understand what the hell he was crying for, I couldn't understand how to feel. "Should I be sorry for him?" "Should I ask what's wrong"? I wasn't sure. So, I just sat there looking at him while he sobbed like a child.

After about ten minutes of this drama, Damien blurted out "you just don't understand. You just don't understand." He continued "I am so tired, I am really tired of it all!" Astonished, I asked the obvious question, "what are you tired of, Damien?" That's when he began recounting tales from his past, shedding light on tumultuous relationships he had experienced.

Disturbingly, he confessed to subjecting all three of his children's mothers to physical abuse during a period when he maintained simultaneous involvement with them. The sheer gravity of the things Damien revealed to me and the impact it had on my emotions left me feeling nauseated, unable to fully comprehend or process the depth of his ability to manipulate so many women during the course of his lifetime.

Although he tried to reassure me that he has since been reformed and has stopped such maladaptive behavior several years now, it was very troubling to hear some of the things he revealed. He was now insisting that I was the first person that he truly felt understood him. And that he was willing to settle down and make this work. He said he knew that he was not perfect but he is willing to try to be a better person for us.

As you might imagine, I found myself in a quandary of emotions at this time. While I did genuinely care for Damien, the disconcerting drama surrounding his past indiscretions raised significant concerns that I could not dismiss. Am I capable of continuing a relationship with someone who carries around such a weighty history? And who appears dismissive of my legitimate apprehensions?

This revelation along with my recent experiences with Damien presented an onerous task, which required careful introspection and consideration on my part. I was too old, too caring, too wise for this entanglement Damien has brought to my life. Without being able to quiet my thoughts and my stomach, I held him and tried to comfort him. I was very concerned at this time, but my concerns went far beyond emotional at this time.

Remember I always thought something didn't sit too right with Damien even from school days? This was my dilemma at this time! Where do we go from this episode, this show that Damien had put down?

In my research, I have learnt that when confronted about their embarrassing behavior and mistreatment of others, the narcissist might employ a manipulative tactic known as "crying for sympathy." They shed tears to portray themselves as remorseful and vulnerable, admitting to past wrongdoings as a way to appear self-aware and seemingly willing to change.

However, this emotional display is often a facade designed to elicit empathy and compassion from others, further positioning themselves as the victim rather than the perpetrator.

By claiming exhaustion and a desire to stop hurting others, they aim to gain understanding and leniency, shifting focus away from their actions and avoiding accountability. Despite the seemingly emotional confession, it is crucial to remain cautious, as narcissists are known for their ability to use perceived emotions as tools for manipulation and self-preservation.

I was unaware of his tactics at the time, so I was easy on him, but began to look at him differently. Something just was not right with this man, but I could not put my finger on it. The foolish thing is that somewhere in between those moments of doubt, I still had a desire for Damien to be the person I wanted him to be. I did not like the reality that was facing me, so I continued to hold on to the fantasy.

After about a week or so in an unexpected twist, Damien went into hibernation. He completely withdrew himself, leaving me hanging and wondering what the heck was going on this time. By this time I was unbothered with Damien and his games, lies and manipulation. I did not call him and neither did he call nor message. This went on for a few days until he showed up at my house unannounced. I was neither happy or angry about it. I just felt nothing at the time.

I did not have the mental capacity to process anything regarding Damien at that time. The torment I went through prior had left me numb. He wanted to talk, so I sat on the porch with him and

I listened. He was apologetic for all that he's put me through and explained that the few days that I did not hear from him, was because he felt so bad when he thought about how our relationship was causing me stress.

He further explained that the mediator was a young person and he could not relate to her, so he just sat there and said nothing throughout the three sessions he and his wife had thus far. When she realized she was not getting through to him, she decided to send their case back to the Magistrate because she was unable to reach him. I was able to relate with the therapist at that time, because I too was fed up with Damien's games, manipulation and indecisiveness.

Damien continued to visit my house, but the overnight stays had ceased. It became apparent to me that he was not making any real progress with his divorce, despite the narrative he had led me to believe. As I began to process the tumultuous experiences I had with this man, it dawned on me how short a time it took for him to have my life in such an emotional disarray. I felt myself withdrawing emotionally, but at the same time some part of me was still hoping that I was wrong about what I was making Damien out to be.

To my dismay, I later discovered that Damien was involved with yet another woman, in addition to Ms. Patsy. The revelation came when I caught him red-handed one night, shortly after he left my home complaining of being tired, but seemingly anxious for some reason.

His restlessness raised a red flag and fuelled my suspicion. Determined to get to the bottom of his haste to leave, I followed him. Only to find him not too far from where I live, in the company of one of the very women he had mentioned during his moments of revelation.

It became clear that Damien never stopped being intimately involved with her over the years. Despite the fact that I was trying to withdraw from Damien during this period, I couldn't help but feel a profound sense of betrayal, hurt, confusion, and manipulation.

Although nervous and filled with anxiety I was adamant to put an end to this web with Damien. But I had to know for sure, so I could convince myself once and for all that I needed to give up on this devious man that I thought I could have loved. I drove until I saw his car and I parked next to it and, I waited for him.

It took him about forty-five minutes before he came strolling to open his car door, with keys in hand. He was so focused that he did not even see me in my car parked next to him. I came out of my car and confronted Damien saying, "I thought you were going home?"

I have to laugh at myself now yes! This was so out of character for me. Only a narcissist can be so effective in sending someone down that emotional path. My reaction was spontaneous and dangerous. Remember, Damien was an instructor in the special forces in the Army that exercised rigorously several times a week, right?

But at that time, all sense of reasoning went out of my head, I rushed up to him, held him by the front collar of his uniform and physically jacked him up. I pushed him onto a nearby wall where we were parked and said to him, "you promised you will never hurt me, Damien!" "You promised!!!"

He looked at me in shock and said, "Girl, you know what you're doing?" "Are you sure you want to get physical with me?" That's when the reality of what I was up against hit me. I walked away and went to my car. As I drove off Damien followed me back home.

When we got to my place, his initial reaction was one of anger, swiftly followed by attempts to shift the blame onto me for catching him in the act. In true narcissistic fashion, he deflected responsibility and pointed fingers at me, insinuating that if I had simply stayed home as he left, I would have been spared the pain and knowledge of his actions. It was a classic display of manipulative tactics aimed at turning the tables and avoiding accountability for his own wrongdoing.

Not aware at the time of the repercussions of this phase in the manipulation cycle of a narcissist, I continued in arguments and fits of rage, and explanations about how he was affecting my mental, and emotional health. I could not carry on with him anymore and I was serious about it. Although I still tried to get some explanation out of him that would close the wounds he had inflicted on every fibre of my being. Damien tried to get me to allow him to stay the night, claiming that he was now too tired to drive home.

I think that level of his manipulation was what did it for me. I flipped and in no uncertain terms I told him it was over between us and that if I ever see him again it would be too soon. The tears began to pour, I truly don't understand where he stores that quantity of tears, that man can cry a literal river of tears, like I've never seen.

When he realised, I was not falling for it, he began to show signs of anger, then he began crying again when he realized the anger was not working while pleading, "Why, babe? Why did you follow me there?" he continued, "You should have just stayed home and watch TV, I left you watching TV, not so?" All because he got caught.

It was painful to acknowledge that the connection I had cherished was built upon a facade, and a psychologically constructed mechanism designed to entrap and control me. Recognizing this truth shattered my perception of Damien and left me grappling with a profound sense of betrayal. I mourned the loss of the person I thought he was, and in its place emerged the stark reality of his true self – devoid of empathy and genuine emotional connection.

The stark contrast between the false facade and the unfeeling reality was a harsh awakening, leaving me with a deep sense of sadness and the need to break free from the emotional entanglement that bound me to him.

Cycle five

It was now ten months and I hadn't been in contact with Damien since the dramatic end to our relationship. During those ten months I experienced hell through my own mind. I swear my brain was on steroids, if that is possible, because the thoughts of what I had experienced with Damien consumed me. Every minute of every day for approximately three of those months was spent researching Damien's behavior and trying to get answers about the way he treated me.

As I researched and began getting some clarity the load began to get lighter. I went from focussing on the debilitating pain I was experiencing to immersing myself in my work and studies.

I managed to achieve the qualifying requisite to travel to two events with my company. The first one was to Jamaica, which was beautiful, other than the odd moments when I found myself in Montego walking on the beach at five thirty in the morning, watching the sun rise on the ocean and thinking to myself, "why did he have to be that way?

He could have been here with me and we could have been so happy, I knew if Damien was different, we would have survived any challenge together. I thought of our song, "Perfect" by Ed Sheeran, we spoke of growing old together and travelling, but this mental illness I was now discovering was a huge obstacle in the fairy tale at the back of my mind.

The thoughts just brought the tears as I sat on one of the beach chairs basking in my sorrowful thoughts amidst the glorious ambience of the ocean, white sands and the chattering sounds of breakfast being prepared in the background of the Rose Hall Hilton.

As I sat there, I saw the figure of a woman coming toward me. Turned out she was attending the same event that I was there for, but she was from Barbados. She had just finished her morning walk on the beach and she thought she'd come over to say, "hello". We introduced ourselves as she sat on the lounge chair next to me and we began chatting.

Somehow, I believe women sense each other's pain, because Marva and I began talking as if we knew each other for several years. Turns out that she too was in a situation with her fiancé and was having a hard time also. We spoke for hours and it was a great release. We soon left to get ready to join our team for breakfast, planning to meet up again at the reggae night on the beach later that evening.

The activities of the next couple days managed to rescue me from my thoughts of despair and it turned out to be a really great trip. That was just the start of a rewarding next few months because I was able to qualify again for an all expenses paid trip to Germany. It was another amazing experience which I will probably tell you about in the next book. (laugh) By that time I was thinking of Damien less each day.

I was comfortable with the knowledge I had found about his personality disorder being the culprit in the relationship and I figured it was time to accept it for what it was and move on. It was not an easy journey, but it was one that I had to take in order to regain my self-worth and continue on the path to the career goals I had been working hard to achieve.

Cycle six

The Pandemic

In 2019, the world was gripped by the pandemic, and everything around us was changing. Life became even more uncertain as we witnessed the increasing number of deaths caused by Covid-19. However, this challenging time instilled in us a stronger determination to appreciate the beauty and gift of life, rather than letting circumstances like what happened with Damien rob us of joy.

Prior to the pandemic, I had achieved a certain level of success in my career. However, the dynamics shifted dramatically due to the restrictions imposed by Covid-19. Visiting clients and meeting new prospects became impossible, prompting me, like many others, to find alternative ways to make a living.

I decided to start a business operating from home, and given the circumstances, I chose an essential service: a take-out restaurant.

With the support of my daughter, we embarked on this venture, which turned out to be a lot of work but also a source of great enjoyment because of the support we received.

To promote our take-out restaurant, I utilized social media by posting pictures of the delicious meals we prepared. The response was overwhelmingly positive, and our business flourished as a result. One day, while my daughter was serving a customer, she returned where I was in the kitchen in a hurry, exclaiming, "Mom, you won't believe who is outside to place an order." Guess who?

Yup! It was Damien! Despite it being a year and two months since we had last seen Damien, the mere thought of him being so close instantly triggered my anxiety. For the next few weeks, Damien became a great supporter of our business. He would interact with me on a more personal level as he placed orders for his colleagues and handled the pick-up and delivery for them.

As time went on, he seemed to grow more comfortable in his interactions. However, I remained cautious because of my prior research on narcissistic personality disorder, (NPD) which I believed explained his maladaptive behavior.

Though I allowed myself to engage with him in a business context, I was careful about my interactions and took his cunning attempts for granted, I thought I had things under control emotionally with Damien by this time. I was soon to find out how wrong I was.

In the months leading up to this, I had consciously avoided reading or learning more about narcissism because it had consumed me in the past. All I wanted to do was let go of the experience with

Damien and move on. And I was succeeding, until he unexpectedly reappeared after a year and two months. Seemingly, without any attempts to "hoover" me at first. This made me begin to question my previous findings, and my questions regarding him being narcissistic.

Dangerous thoughts started creeping into my mind, contemplating whether I had been wrong about him. I found myself increasingly tempted to speak with him about what I had discovered.

As Damien grew more comfortable, he would sometimes order dinner and ate it on my porch before leaving. I couldn't bring myself to ask him to stop, so instead, I decided to have a conversation with him. It turned out to be a big mistake, as I underestimated the power of a master manipulator like him.

Cycle seven

My Birthday

My birthday was coming up and it was recognized that I was really working hard running this new-found business. It was growing and I needed a little break. I had mentioned that to Damien in one of our conversations and he quickly offered to take me to Mon Rivere for the weekend of my birthday.

He was swift to say, "no strings attached eh mam." He was so cunning and waited for the right opportunity. He knew I love Mon Rivere and he chose the right time to make this proposal.

Knowing what I know and how things turned out in the past I was very sceptical. But these people have a certain type of charisma and power of persuasion that just eats at your core. What you think happened next?

Soon I was like a kid in a candy store preparing for my birthday weekend to Mon Rivere with Damien. As mentioned, it was a year and a half and I believed I had things under control. I was not in a relationship with anyone and I was doing my thing and at peace with myself.

So, if I allowed Damien to influence me in any sort of intimacy that would be my burden to bear. But I believed I was strong enough to resist him in that way and just enjoy having some form of company for my birthday.

We went to Mon Rivere, it was really amazing. The rain was pouring on the way there and it was night time. It was a little challenging with the winding roads, no street lights and ongoing road works did not make it any easier. But we arrived at our destination just after eleven, in time to get changed and start the birthday celebration at midnight. The environment was not in my favour, because it was difficult to say no to Damien, although I know it was the sensible thing to do.

As a matter of fact, we went with my van so I drove, but would you believe that on the way I had so many thoughts of turning back it wasn't funny. But the temptation to have a relaxing weekend in Mon Rivere for my birthday was extremely difficult to pass up. Damien or no Damien!

When we got up the following morning we prepared to go for breakfast. The ambience was perfect! The morning air was crisp, the swimming pool was right outside our room and the water was still resembling a bed of glass. The trees were green and lush from the dew that was visible as the sun came up.

167

The chirping of the birds was heavenly! Our host had a pot of bush tea awaiting as he sat under the shade of a big mango tree.

Damien and I both drank some of the tea which smelled like mint and something or the other, but it was lovely! We were then told that it was cannabis and mint. This was a first, Damien and I looked at each other and laughed. He was not used to this either.

Anyway, breakfast was ready and we were invited to the kitchen area to dine. There was homemade bread, pancakes, saltfish, sausages and eggs and other local dishes to choose from. The meal was divine. After we ate, we decided to go for a walk on the beach.

While we were on the beach something happened while I was gathering some unusual stones to take home. There were corals washed up on shore and I wanted some of those also. While gathering these monuments of my Mon Rivere trip, Damien walked behind me helping me to identify the best ones.

We both began laughing and actually identifying characters in the stones. One looked like a wolf, the other like an elephant and so on. We began laughing hysterically, the feeling was uncontrollable. We laughed until we cried and then in between the laughter we realized that the tea had given us a buzz. We were high! (lol) It was a crazy moment that I smile at even now that I'm writing about it.

When we got back to the hotel, Damien got quiet. We showered and laid on the bed to take a nap and he just got quiet. I asked what was wrong and he didn't answer for a few minutes. I felt the bed shaking a bit and I took my stare from the Television on the wall to him on the bed next to me.

Damien's face was wet with tears and he was shaking like a leaf. I asked what was wrong, once again and he began sobbing loudly! I got so scared, I held him and kept asking what was wrong.

After he got his composure a bit, he began to explain that he never meant to hurt me the way he did. He said that the last year and a half without even being able to speak to me was torture. That he wants to make a commitment to me and he does not want to lose us this time. He lamented about his situation at home and that he was over with everyone because he was getting older and the love we had was like nothing he ever experienced before and he wants that back.

I listened to Damien and I compared what I had discovered about narcissism and I got scared. "Was this thing I had discovered so real? Was it really playing out before my very eyes, or was Damien genuine?" I tried to explain to Damien what I had discovered about narcissistic personality disorder in detail this time.

He listened closely and began to cry again asking me if I can please help him because he doesn't understand why he is the way he is. As the empath that I am, I actually fell for it and was roped back into Damien's web of lies and deceit once again.

One of the reasons why a narcissist is so effective in their cycle of manipulation is because they actually believe their own lies. Narcissism will go to any length to gain the object of its desire. And that is exactly what we are to them, "objects".

After we left Mon Rivere, things went seemingly well for a few weeks. We had a wedding coming up in the family and Damien was excited to attend. He gifted the bride and groom with some money and he appeared so genuine. I actually began to think that there was hope after all for Damien and me but, I was still not totally convinced.

On the day of the wedding, he was late for the church, I was a bit distracted because I kept looking out for him. After the ceremony and the photo shoot we headed to the reception. Things were going so smoothly, but it didn't last, again. While at the reception, Damien kept playing with his phone. It was so obvious that he was pre-occupied in front of everyone, that it made me a little embarrassed.

Not too long after that scenario, Damien left the reception to take a phone call, appearing very anxious as his phone rang. He was on the outside of the building, and he was on the phone for a while. When he returned, I asked if everything was okay.

He watched me and said, "this girl wouldn't stop calling me." I was in disbelief! I deliberately didn't ask about Ms. Patsy because I believed that after a year and a half and that dramatic episode in Mon Rivere, that that situation was a thing of the past.

Apparently, I gave Damien too much credit. His wife was out of the country for a while because I guess she had too much of his crap to deal with and needed a break or a permanent get away. But he continued to play his games nonetheless.

Of course, Damien denied being still involved with the young lady and I didn't believe him. But you know what, I was tired! I was not doing this no more. I didn't fuss, I just accepted it for whatever it was and didn't ask any more questions. Was I hurting?

Cycle Eight

The mask falls off

At this point I don't know if it was hurt because of the way Damien constantly betrayed and lied to me, or if it was the pain of being stripped of my dignity. Whatever it was it didn't feel as though it mattered anymore. I was still very perplexed and couldn't figure out how to describe this part of my journey with Damien. I just knew that I couldn't continue like that, this is not what I had signed up for.

One week after the wedding Damien began to withdraw, the text messages slowed down again. The phone calls became less and the same cycle that was now too familiar began. I was really okay with it and began preparing myself mentally and emotionally to deal with the impending outcome.

There were times I reflected on Damien's revelation of his past and wondered if I were to have a conversation with these women, "What would they say about him?" All three of his 'baby mamas' had migrated at one point. Many years ago, after one of them left Damien, she ended up living with a female companion in the US, with his two boys. Sadly, she became an alcoholic and eventually passed away. Damien got the news when he was at my house.

I've never seen someone try so hard to cry. It was not convincing at all. But I had to remind myself that this guy is probably a narcissist. They have no empathy. I began to pay closer attention to Damien's behavior after that episode as I resumed my research on the topic, more earnest this time.

Two weeks had passed and I was barely getting a text from Damien. During that time, I was getting more engrossed in the study of narcissism. I kept comparing what I had been through and what I was learning. The similarities made me cushion myself for the acceptance that this was never going to work. This time I dug deeper into the scientific study of human behavior and it was intriguing.

A little after two weeks of this new found hobby of mine, Damien shows up at my door with a bag of what is called in narcissistic term "bread crumb". In narcissistic terms, "breadcrumbing" refers to a manipulative tactic used by narcissists to maintain control and keep their victims engaged in the relationship. It is a form of emotional manipulation where the narcissist sporadically sends small, seemingly positive or affectionate messages or actions to their target, just like leaving breadcrumbs for someone to follow.

The purpose of breadcrumbing is to give the victim a glimmer of hope or attention, making them feel valued and desired. However, these breadcrumbs are usually inconsistent and inadequate, leaving the victim craving more and seeking validation from the narcissist. This behavior keeps the victim emotionally invested and bound to the narcissist while the narcissist maintains power and control in the relationship.

That evening, Damien looked like he'd been having a hard time. He looked miserable, he needed a hair cut and he appear tired. He was due to retire in few days and a function was being planned. In as much as I seem to be the fitting one in the matrix, he came to invite me to his retirement function. I felt a little touched, but I was cautious because of my further findings and the comparisons I was making with this personality disorder I was suspecting Damien of having.

With the gifts he brought and the invitation to his function, Damien took his overnight bag out of his car. And made his way very casually into my room to rest it down. He came back out on the porch where I was sitting and I tried to have a conversation with him about what has been happening for the past two weeks.

He summed it up to be the stress of retirement and not being certain what he'll do now. After all this was his life for over thirty-six years. I guessed that's why he appeared so miserable. Learning that narcissists don't do well with life's transitions, helped me to understand Damien's demeanour somewhat.

You see, retirement poses unique challenges for narcissists, whose identity and self-worth are often intricately linked to their professional achievements and the admiration they receive from others. The prospect of losing the status and control they once held in their career can be unsettling for a narcissist, leading to feelings of insecurity and a crisis identity.

As retirement approaches, they may attempt to secure alternative sources of narcissistic supply to compensate for the decreasing attention and validation they receive. Engaging in grandiose storytelling about their past accomplishments or seeking new avenues for praise and recognition may become common strategies.

During retirement, narcissists may face difficulties adjusting to a lower profile and decreased attention, leading them to assert their significance in other ways. They may employ control tactics in personal relationships, intensifying manipulative behaviors to maintain dominance and ensure their needs for admiration and attention are met. Financial matters can also pose challenges, particularly if a narcissist hasn't adequately planned for retirement or faces financial constraints.

Moreover, some narcissists may idealize their past and reminisce about their career successes while disregarding any failures, as a way to uphold their self-aggrandizing narrative and maintain a sense of self-importance. When I learnt of this, it became clear why Damien spent so much time in the love bombing stage, showing me all those pictures of his achievement and, other accolades.

I looked at him and I felt sorry for him, because what I was understanding was in alignment with Damien's personality. It was so on point! Anyhow, Damien obviously came with the intention to stay for the night. I allowed him and we had a pleasant night.

We spoke a lot about a lot of things and I think I was at the point of conducting a "behavioral analysis" on Damien. I was studying him to understand the relevance of what I was learning without him knowing what I was doing. I explained some of my findings to him though, he just did not realise that he was the subject of my studies.

My phone rang around six in the morning, I had just opened my eyes. I tried answering it but the person hung up. I found it strange so I showed him the number on my phone and asked if he'd recognized it. Hmmmm, well that certainly was not the right

thing to do that hour of the morning, Damien responded, "you start with that foolishness this hour of the morning?", he continued, "How I supposed to know who is that? Is your phone the person called." I was startled at his response and the manner in which he answered.

This made me call the number to find out who it was. The person did not answer. My anxiety started to raise. Anyway, his phone rang and guess who? Ms Patsy! Video calling him to see where he was. I watched him and laughed.

Damien sat on a stool at the end of the bed while on the phone with Ms Patsy as she ranted and raved about how he is a liar and that he told her our relationship was over two weeks ago. The whole call was just too much.

When he was through with the drama, I asked him, with no emotions, "how do you feel?" He shrugged his shoulders as if to say, no how. I said to him, "you know how I feel?" he looked at me with that familiar look of nothingness in his eyes. I said to him, "do you remember when we were in Mon Rivere and I told you I'll try to help you?" he said "yes." I said and I also told you that you will never be able to hurt me again?" he said "yes." I then said "well this is what I meant. You know why?" Because I feel nothing but pity for you at this point.

I am not hurt I am not disappointed; I just feel nothing but pity. I said, "Damien you are destroying yourself and the people that care for you, you need help or you will end up alone, angry and sad in your older years. He just stared at me and began to cry, again!!

As the veil of Damien's narcissistic traits was lifted, he found himself backed into a corner with nowhere to hide. He appeared fatigued, unable to muster the usual defences he relied upon. Caught red-handed, he had no plausible excuses or ways to deflect blame. In response, he retreated into a state of silence, refusing to engage or address the accusations against him. The once confident and manipulative demeanour he exuded crumbled, leaving behind a vulnerable and exposed individual.

I tell my story because no abuser is silencing me! If my story can save one person or help them to understand that narcissistic abuse or narcissism is real, I would have done my part.

I just left the room and told him to organize his things, because this will be the last time, he will ever set foot in my home. Damien looked the worst I've ever seen him, but it helped me in several ways, mainly by fully understanding the effects that narcissistic personality disorder from a first-hand experience, a real vantage point.

It was an expensive lesson but one well learnt, and one that I will not let go to waste. I was able to see his narcissistic veil fall off and it was pathetic to witness.

My experience with Damien was a painful process, but it also marked the beginning of my journey towards healing and reclaiming my own identity.

I've learned to recognize the illusions of perceived personalities or false selves and prioritize my own well-being and emotional health. I've learned to set clear boundaries and continue educating myself on this journey. It is the only way liberate oneself on this path.

"Turn your wounds into wisdom."
Oprah Winfrey

Chapter Ten

Summary of My Story

Upon examining Damien's character and considering certain aspects of his upbringing, I discovered there was indeed a genetic predisposition towards narcissism. His father, a bodybuilder who fathered over fifteen children at a young age, did not live past the age of forty-one. Damien was just under two years when his father died of a massive heart attack, leaving behind a complicated family dynamic.

Furthermore, Damien's exposure to a tumultuous environment, constantly moving from one relative to another, combined with his mother's history as an outpatient of a mental institution, provided fertile ground for the development of narcissistic traits.

Adding to this foundation, Damien's extensive military career spanning over thirty-six years likely fuelled his narcissism, perpetuating the cycle of manipulation throughout the years. Understanding the dynamics of this personality disorder, alongside my personal experience with Damien, led me to the conclusion that I had firsthand experience with a narcissist.

Rather than harbouring resentment, I found myself feeling sympathy for Damien, as it became clear that much of his behavior was not intentional. He is simply wired differently. Many individuals who struggle with this disorder may not fully comprehend the reasons behind their actions, but taking the time to examine their roots and genetic predispositions can offer valuable insight and encourage them to seek professional help.

Not all personality disorders are beyond repair. It all depends on the degree of the affliction and it all begins with self-awareness. The challenge with that is getting someone with narcissistic tendency to admit that there's a problem with their behavior, since the narcissism protects them.

While doing the research, I developed a keen interest in the scientific study of human behavior, with a deliberate focus on this complex mechanism. It has certainly provided me with a deeper insight into narcissism, allowing me to view Damien's actions with compassion.

I also recognize the importance of embracing the knowledge and raising awareness of these disorders. Although I felt an overwhelming amount of sympathy for Damien, it will never be enough to be drawn back into his matrix. When one acquires this type of knowledge, one has to use discernment.

The next mind-boggling realization was that I was learning about myself as well, not just Damien's characteristics. Now I was even more intrigued, because I began to understand why I tolerated Damien's disrespect even though he had crossed all of my boundaries. And also, why I remained hopeful despite all of the ills I was experiencing. I will delve deeper into this in edition two of "Narcissism Has No Face."

Damien was never professionally diagnosed, that is as far as I know, but during one of his hoover attempts, he did mention that he understood what I was saying about personality disorders. He claimed to be following me on my platform and that he did some research on his own.

He said it allowed him to do some introspection and he agrees that he does have a problem. But then he asked me why I did not help him instead of abandoning him the way I did. (I went totally no contact at the end of the relationship). That was the turning point in the short conversation with Damien, he got that far because he called from a number I did not recognize!

That was enough to convince me that narcissistic individuals would do or say whatever is necessary, in order to regain control of their victim.

My journey from victim to survivor is a testament to the strength of resilience and the transformative power of knowledge. By shedding light on the tactics deployed by those afflicted with this disorder, we can provide hope and healing to those who have endured the devaluation stage and break the cycle of narcissistic abuse.

I am grateful for my story, because out of my pain I was able to give birth to the TTNAWH Foundation.

Many persons can now turn to us for answers and support if they are having similar experiences that may be caused by narcissistic entrapment.

The manipulative tactic of hoovering, employed to achieve dominance and control over a victim that may have slipped out of the narcissist's control, can be hugely effective. It has proven to be a challenging and emotional task for many. Setting boundaries and prioritizing your well-being along with awareness is crucial to you successfully resisting these attempts.

This is because when a narcissist is successful at ensnaring someone, especially if the fuel is potent, they never give up on you. It is said that because of the composition of narcissism, the afflicted one believes they own you for the rest of your life. Damien still tries to contact me from time to time, but I am weaponized against his attempts.

Narcissists are everywhere! I am now compelled to share my story with the world, as it is crucial for people to understand the profound truth: if we neglect to tend to our wounds and take the necessary steps toward healing, they will fester within, gradually consuming us from the inside.

It is my earnest belief that this message needs to reach countless individuals who may be silently suffering, empowering them to embark on their own journey of healing and transformation. With the help of the TTNAWH Foundation, we can guide you to awareness and grant you a measure of support to you on this profound path. It is a challenging journey but with the right mindset you can overcome it.

Damien eventually reached out to one of my relatives and when she gave him the encouragement he needed, she was then used as his "flying monkey" – a term commonly used to describe individuals who, either willingly or unknowingly, support and enable the narcissist's manipulative behaviors. They are usually used to keep abreast with their victim's lifestyle or developments to ascertain an opportunistic time to hoover the one that escaped them. (See below for a better understanding of *Flying Monkeys and Enablers*).

Please be aware that the illustrative story shared here is intended solely to help you understand the characteristics of narcissism. It is not meant to cause offense or defame any specific individual. The story has been presented for educational purposes and should not be construed as a representation of real events or individuals. Any resemblance to actual persons or situations is purely coincidental.

Flying Monkeys and Enablers

Enablers are individuals who, knowingly or unknowingly, support and enable the narcissist's abusive behavior. They may provide validation, make excuses, or actively participate in the manipulation and control tactics employed by the narcissist. Enablers may be family members, friends, or even colleagues who are either unaware of the abuse or choose to turn a blind eye to it.

Flying monkeys, on the other hand, refer to individuals who are recruited or manipulated by the narcissist to carry out their bidding. They act as extensions of the narcissist, assisting in their schemes, spreading misinformation, or engaging in targeted harassment against the narcissist's victims.

Flying monkeys are often used by narcissists to further isolate and intimidate their victims, creating a network of support for their abusive behavior.

Both enablers and flying monkeys play significant roles in perpetuating the cycle of narcissistic abuse. It is important for victims and those supporting them to recognize the presence of enablers and flying monkeys in order to break free from the manipulation and seek the necessary support and healing.

Why do Narcissists get Married?

If I had to give a single answer to this question it would be to have a constant supply of narcissistic fuel. But it is a little more complex than that, but I know by now that you won't expect less than complexity when it comes to narcissism, right?

Narcissists may get married for various reasons, although their motivations can be different from those of individuals with healthier relationship goals. Here are a few possible reasons why narcissists might choose to get married:

- **Narcissistic Fuel:** Narcissists thrive on attention, admiration, and validation from others. Getting married can provide a consistent source of narcissistic fuel, as they can receive admiration and attention from their spouse. In addition, the unsuspecting spouse may be used for character traits, residual benefits and a primary source of this fuel. The spouse is like a safe source of fuel.

- **Social Status and Image:** Marriage is often seen as a societal norm and can contribute to the narcissist's desired image of success, stability, and respectability. It allows them to present themselves as desirable and accomplished individuals.

- **Control and Manipulation:** Narcissists may see marriage as an opportunity to assert control and manipulate their partner. They may use marriage as a means to dominate, exploit, and manipulate their spouse's emotions, actions, and decisions.

- **External Validation:** Some narcissists seek external validation to bolster their fragile self-esteem. By being married, they can use their marital status as proof of their worthiness and desirability to others.

- **Idealization and Devaluation Cycle:** In the early stages of a relationship, narcissists often idealize their partner, showering them with love, attention, and affection. Marriage can be a way to solidify this idealization. However, as the relationship progresses, the narcissist may transition into devaluation, undermining their spouse's self-esteem and asserting power and control over them.

It is not cast in stone that all persons afflicted with this disorder will choose to get married, and their motivations may vary. Additionally, entering a relationship with a narcissist can be challenging and emotionally damaging. Hence the importance of equipping yourself upfront with knowledge from a trusted source in this regard. It's crucial to be aware of the red flags and seek support if you suspect you are in a relationship with a narcissist.

When it comes to cheating on their spouses, there can be several underlying factors that contribute to this behavior. Here are some possible explanations:

- **Need for Validation and Attention:** Narcissists have an insatiable need for validation, admiration, and attention. While marriage can provide a certain level of validation, some narcissists may still seek additional external sources of attention and validation, which can lead them to engage in infidelity.

- **Sense of Entitlement**: Narcissists often have a strong sense of entitlement and believe that they deserve special treatment. They may view monogamy as restrictive and feel entitled to pursue other partners, disregarding the commitment and loyalty expected in a marriage.

- **Lack of Empathy and Emotional Connection:** Narcissists struggle with empathy and have difficulty forming deep emotional connections. They may view their spouse as merely a source of narcissistic supply, and when their needs are not being met or they become bored, they may seek excitement or emotional gratification through extramarital affairs.

- **Power and Control**: Cheating can also be a way for narcissists to exert power and control over their spouse. By engaging in infidelity, they undermine their partner's self-esteem and create a power dynamic where they hold the upper hand.

- **Impulsivity and Thrill-Seeking Behavior:** Some narcissists are prone to impulsive and thrill-seeking behavior. They may engage in cheating as a way to fulfil their need for excitement, novelty, and risk-taking, disregarding the potential consequences to their marriage. Narcissists hardly ever initiate a divorce or separation unless, the character traits and residual benefits of their new supply are far more superior than that of the primary source at home.

Although infidelity is very common amongst this kind, not all narcissists engage in infidelity, and not all instances of infidelity are perpetrated by narcissists. However, the lack of empathy, emotional connection, and the constant pursuit of narcissistic fuel can make narcissists more prone to such behavior.

"Within your healing journey lies the power to shift your vibration. As you release what no longer serves you, you make room for the energy of well-being to flow abundantly. Trust in your ability to align with healing, and watch as your reality transforms in beautiful harmony."

Sue Barker

Chapter Eleven
Healing from Narcissistic Abuse

Healing from narcissistic abuse is a challenging and deeply personal journey that requires time, self-reflection, and self-care. Here are some steps that may assist in the healing process:

Acknowledge the abuse: Recognize and accept that you have experienced narcissistic abuse. This involves understanding the manipulative tactics, gaslighting, and emotional manipulation employed by the narcissistic individual.

Seek support: Reach out to trusted friends, family, or a support group who can provide empathy, validation, and understanding. Sharing your experiences with others who have gone through similar situations can be immensely helpful in the healing process.

Set boundaries: Establish clear boundaries to protect yourself from further harm. This may involve limiting or cutting off contact with the narcissistic individual, particularly if they continue to engage in abusive behaviors.

Focus on self-care: Prioritize your well-being and engage in activities that bring you joy and promote healing. This may include practicing self-care routines, engaging in therapy or counselling, participating in mindfulness exercises, and nurturing healthy relationships.

Rebuild self-esteem: Narcissistic abuse often erodes self-esteem and self-worth. Engage in self-reflection and remind yourself of your inherent value. Challenge negative self-beliefs and replace them with positive affirmations. Surround yourself with supportive and uplifting individuals who appreciate you for who you are.

Educate yourself: Learn about Narcissistic Personality Disorder and the dynamics of narcissistic abuse. This knowledge can help you gain insight into the manipulative tactics used by narcissists and validate your own experiences.

Process your emotions: Allow yourself to experience and process the range of emotions that arise from the abuse. This may include anger, grief, sadness, confusion, and betrayal. Seek therapy or counselling to work through these emotions in a safe and supportive environment.

Practice self-forgiveness: It's common for survivors of narcissistic abuse to blame themselves or question their own actions. Remember that you are not responsible for the abuser's behavior. Practice self-compassion and forgive yourself for any perceived mistakes or shortcomings.

Set realistic expectations: Healing takes time, and the journey is not linear. Be patient and kind to yourself as you navigate the ups and downs of recovery. Celebrate small victories and recognize that healing is a gradual process.

Reclaim your power: Rediscover your identity, strengths, and passions. Focus on personal growth and empowerment. Surround yourself with positive influences that support your journey toward healing and reclaiming your life.

NARCISSISM HAS NO FACE

Remember, healing from narcissistic abuse is unique to each individual, and there is no one-size-fits-all approach. It's important to prioritize your well-being and seek professional help if needed.

Self-care after Narcissistic Abuse

Self-care is essential for healing and recovering from narcissistic abuse. Here are some self-care practices that can be helpful:

- **Set Boundaries:** Establish and enforce healthy boundaries to protect yourself from further harm. Clearly define what acceptable and unacceptable behavior from others are and communicate your boundaries assertively.

- **Practice Self-Compassion:** Be kind and understanding towards yourself. Recognize that the abuse was not your fault and that you deserve love, care, and respect. Treat yourself with compassion and nurture your emotional well-being.

- **Seek Support:** Reach out to trusted friends, family, or support groups who can provide a safe space for you to share your experiences and emotions. Consider therapy or counselling with a professional experienced in trauma and abuse to help you navigate the healing process.

- **Practice Mindfulness and Self-Reflection:** Engage in activities that promote self-awareness and self-reflection, such as meditation, journaling, or therapy. Develop a deeper understanding of yourself, your needs, and your values.

- **Prioritize Your Well-being:** Make your physical and mental health a priority. Engage in activities that bring you joy and promote relaxation, such as exercise, creative outlets, or spending time in nature.

- **Establish a Supportive Routine:** Create a routine that incorporates self-care activities and healthy habits. This can include regular exercise, adequate sleep, nutritious meals, and activities that promote relaxation and stress reduction.

- **Practice Emotional Healing:** Explore techniques such as therapy, support groups, or self-help resources that focus on healing emotional wounds, rebuilding self-esteem, and developing healthier relationships.

- **Practice Self-Validation:** Learn to trust your own feelings, thoughts, and instincts. Validate your experiences and emotions, and remind yourself that your perception of reality is valid.

- **Limit Contact:** If possible, establish distance or limit contact with the narcissistic abuser to protect yourself and aid in your healing process. This may involve setting clear boundaries or, in extreme cases, implementing no-contact or low-contact strategies.

- **Educate Yourself:** Learn about narcissistic abuse, its effects, and recovery. Knowledge can empower you, provide validation, and help you recognize and avoid similar dynamics in the future.

Remember, healing from narcissistic abuse is a journey that takes time and patience. Be gentle with yourself and allow yourself to heal at your own pace. If you find the process overwhelming, don't hesitate to seek professional support.

Coping mechanisms

Unhealthy Coping Mechanisms

Earlier I touched on some coping mechanisms to make the comparison of Narcissism being one such mechanism. These mechanisms can vary from person to person depending on a variety of components, based on the circumstances of the individual. But as a guide, I will list some potentially unhealthy coping mechanisms that some victims of narcissistic abuse might employ to render some relief. You need to pay close attention and seek professional help if you notice the signs of these in yourself or a loved one:

- **Isolation:** The victim might withdraw from friends, family, and social activities, feeling like they can't trust others or fear judgment.

- **Denial or Minimization:** The victim may downplay or ignore the abuse, convincing themselves that it's not as bad as it seems or blaming themselves for the abuser's behavior.

- **Substance Abuse:** Some individuals may turn to alcohol, drugs, or other substances as a way to numb their emotions or escape from the pain.

- **Self-Harm:** In extreme cases, some victims might resort to self-harm as a way to cope with emotional pain or regain a sense of control.

- **Emotional Eating:** Using food as a source of comfort, leading to unhealthy eating habits and potential weight issues.

- **Avoidance:** The person might avoid dealing with their feelings or confronting the abuse, hoping that it will go away on its own.

- **Excessive People-Pleasing:** Trying to please the narcissistic abuser at all costs, sacrificing their own needs and well-being to avoid conflict.

- **Escapism:** Engaging in excessive TV watching, gaming, or other forms of distraction to avoid facing reality.

- **Self-Blame:** The victim might internalize the abuser's messages and believe they deserve the mistreatment.

- **Engaging in further Destructive Relationships:** Repeating patterns of abusive relationships, or seeking out further relationships without realizing their ability to attract toxic connections.

- **Perfectionism:** Striving for perfection as a way to gain approval or avoid criticism.

- **Compulsive Lying:** The person might resort to lying or making excuses to protect the abuser or avoid confrontations.

It's essential to understand that these coping mechanisms are not healthy or sustainable ways of dealing with narcissistic abuse. Encouraging the individual to seek support from friends, family, or professional counsellors can be beneficial in helping them navigate their emotions and begin the healing process. If you know someone who is experiencing narcissistic abuse, it's crucial to be supportive, empathetic, and encourage them to seek professional help if needed.

Healthy Coping Mechanisms

Healthy coping mechanisms I recommend that have worked for me on my journey. These will provide constructive ways to manage stress and emotional challenges:

- **Seeking Support:** Reach out to friends, family, or support groups to share experiences and emotions in a safe and understanding environment.

- **Setting Boundaries:** Learn to establish and enforce personal boundaries to protect oneself from further abuse.

- **Therapy and Counselling:** Seek professional therapy or counselling to work through the emotional impact of the abuse and develop healthy coping strategies.

- **Journaling:** Write down thoughts and feelings in a journal to gain insights, release emotions, and track progress.

- **Physical Activity:** Engage in regular exercise or physical activities like walking, yoga, or sports to reduce stress and boost mood through the release of endorphins.

- **Mindfulness and Meditation:** Practice mindfulness and meditation to center oneself, reduce anxiety, and promote self-awareness.

- **Creative Expression:** Channel emotions through art, music, writing, or any other creative outlet.

- **Educating Oneself:** Learn about narcissistic abuse and its effects, as knowledge can empower and validate the survivor's experiences.

- **Self-Care:** Prioritize self-care activities like taking relaxing baths, spending time in nature, or doing activities that bring joy and relaxation.

- **Positive Affirmations:** Repeat positive affirmations to challenge negative self-beliefs and foster self-compassion.

- **Healthy Distractions:** Engage in hobbies and things that interests you, or activities that provide enjoyment and distraction from negative thoughts.

- **Practicing Assertiveness:** Learn to assert needs and stand up for oneself in a calm and confident manner.

- **Supportive Community:** Surround oneself with caring and understanding individuals who uplift and validate the survivor's experiences.

- **Limit Contact with Abuser:** If possible, create distance from the narcissistic abuser to minimize further harm.

- **Focus on Future Goals:** Set and work towards personal goals, building a sense of purpose and direction.

Remember that healing from narcissistic abuse is a gradual process, and it's okay to take things one step at a time. I implore you to be patient and gentle with yourselves as you navigate your path to recovery. If you or someone you know is struggling with the effects of narcissistic abuse, seeking professional help can be crucial in facilitating healing and growth.

Chapter Twelve
Finding Love After Narcissistic Abuse
(Is it possible?)

Finding love after narcissistic abuse can be a challenging but ultimately rewarding journey. Here are some steps and considerations for finding healthy love and rebuilding trust:

- **Self-Reflection and Healing:** Before seeking a new relationship, take time to heal and focus on yourself. Engage in self-care, therapy, and self-reflection to address any lingering emotional wounds and build a strong foundation of self-love and self-worth.

- **Set Boundaries:** Establish clear boundaries and standards for how you deserve to be treated in a relationship. Learn to recognize and assertively communicate your needs, wants, and limits. Boundaries are crucial for protecting yourself from potential abusive dynamics.

- **Red Flags Awareness:** Educate yourself about the red flags and warning signs of Narcissistic behavior. Learn from your past experiences and, develop a keen sense of awareness to identify unhealthy patterns or manipulative behaviors in potential partners.

- **Take It Slow:** When entering a new relationship, take it slow and allow trust to build gradually. Healthy relationships are built on trust, respect, and open communication. Give yourself time to observe the other person's character and intentions.

- **Seek Support:** Surround yourself with a strong support system of friends, family, or support groups who understand your journey and can offer guidance and encouragement. They can provide an outside perspective and help you navigate the complexities of dating again.

- **Practice Self-Love:** Prioritize self-love and self-care throughout your dating journey. Treat yourself with kindness, engage in activities you enjoy, and nourish your mind, body, and spirit. Remember that you deserve love and happiness.

- **Communication and Trust:** Open and honest communication is vital in any relationship. Develop trust by sharing your experiences and concerns with your new partner. Pay attention to how they respond and respect your boundaries and emotions.

- **Take Time for Evaluation:** Assess the potential partner's behavior and actions over time. Are they consistent, respectful, and supportive? Do they acknowledge and validate your feelings? Trust your instincts and evaluate whether the relationship aligns with your values and emotional well-being.

Remember, healing from narcissistic abuse takes time, and it's important to prioritize your well-being above all else. Be patient and kind to yourself as you embark on the journey of finding healthy love.

The Aging Narcissist

The aging narcissist refers to a person with narcissistic traits or narcissistic personality disorder (NPD) who is growing older. As individuals age, their personality traits and behaviors can evolve, including those associated with narcissism. Here are some key aspects to consider regarding the aging narcissist:

- **Diminished Energy and Grandiosity:** As narcissists age, they may experience a decline in physical energy and vitality. This can result in a reduction of their grandiose behavior and the need for constant admiration. They may become more focused on preserving their self-image and maintaining control over their surroundings.

- **Fear of Losing Control:** Aging can be challenging for narcissists as it may bring about a loss of physical attractiveness, power, or achievements. This fear of losing control can intensify their need for attention, validation, and admiration. They may engage in behaviors to compensate for their perceived decline and assert dominance over others.

- **Increased Vulnerability and Isolation:** Aging can make narcissists more susceptible to feelings of vulnerability and insecurity. They may struggle with the realization that they are not as invincible or superior as they once believed. This can lead to increased isolation, as they may withdraw from relationships or avoid situations that challenge their ego.

- **Entitlement and Demanding Behavior:** The aging narcissist may exhibit a heightened sense of entitlement and demanding behavior. They may expect special treatment, exploit others' compassion, or use manipulation tactics to meet their aging and maintain a sense of control.

- **Difficulty Adapting to Change:** Narcissists often struggle with adaptability and accepting change, including the physical and emotional changes that come with aging. They may resist or deny the reality of their aging process, clinging to past accomplishments and appearances.

- **Impact on Relationships:** Aging narcissists may struggle to maintain healthy relationships as their self-centred tendencies persist. They may struggle with empathy, struggle to recognize others' needs and engage in controlling or manipulative behaviors. This can strain their relationships with family members, friends, and romantic partners.

It's important to note that while some individuals with narcissistic traits may experience a mellowing or reduction in certain narcissistic behaviors as they age, others may become more entrenched in their narcissistic patterns. Each individual is unique, and the impact of aging on narcissistic traits can vary.

If you are dealing with an aging narcissist in your life, it's crucial to prioritize your own well-being and set appropriate boundaries. Seeking support from therapists, support groups, or counsellors who specialize in narcissistic abuse can be beneficial in navigating these complex dynamics.

Have you ever asked yourself, "Am I a narcissist"?

If you find yourself questioning whether you might be a narcissist, it's a positive sign that you have self-awareness and are open to self-reflection. However, it's important to approach this question with caution and consider seeking professional help or guidance to receive an accurate assessment.

NARCISSISM HAS NO FACE

Narcissistic Personality Disorder (NPD) is a complex mental health condition characterized by a pervasive pattern of grandiosity, a constant need for admiration, and a lack of empathy for others. A diagnosis of NPD can only be made by a qualified mental health professional based on a thorough evaluation of your symptoms and behaviors.

Keep in mind that many people may exhibit some narcissistic traits or behaviors from time to time, but this does not necessarily mean they have NPD. It's normal to have moments of self-centeredness or desire for recognition. However, it becomes a concern when these traits significantly impact your relationships, functioning, and overall well-being.

If you are genuinely concerned about your behavior or the impact it has on others, consider the following steps:

- **Self-Reflection:** Take time to reflect on your thoughts, feelings, and behaviors. Consider how you interact with others, how you respond to criticism or feedback, and your ability to empathize with others.

- **Seek Professional Help:** Consult with a mental health professional, such as a therapist or psychologist, who can provide an objective evaluation and help you gain clarity. They can assess your symptoms, explore underlying factors, and guide you toward appropriate treatment or support.

- **Be Open to Feedback:** Listen to feedback from trusted friends, family, or loved ones who can provide a different perspective on your behavior. Their observations can help you gain insights and understand how your actions impact others.

- **Learn and Grow:** Whether or not you receive a diagnosis of NPD, focusing on personal growth and self-improvement is essential. Engage in self-development activities, such as therapy, counselling, or support groups, to address any problematic patterns, develop healthier relationships, and enhance self-awareness.

Remember, seeking professional guidance is crucial for an accurate assessment and guidance on any potential narcissistic tendencies.

Hope for the Afflicted

Is there hope for someone who suffers from NPD? The answer is not as straightforward as we would like, but there is a measure of hope. However, it will be dependent on a few integral disciplines beginning with self-awareness! But how do you make a narcissist become self-aware if narcissism protects them from believing that something is wrong with them?

Remember the experiment from the American Psychological Association mentioned earlier, that compared the presence or lack thereof of the "grey matter and the "white matter" in the brain? Some schools of thought suggest that there may be ways to increase the presence, of these two bodies of tissues that may be able to assist persons afflicted with this condition to respond to cognitive therapy.

Though very challenging, there may be a possibility for narcissists to soften deeply ingrained patterns of behavior, experience personal growth and develop healthier ways of relating to others.

The first approach towards any type of change would be self-awareness. Recognizing and acknowledging one's narcissistic tendencies or the impact of NPD is crucial. Also crucial to this turnaround is diet and exercise. Meditation can be very calming and allows the central nervous system a measure of detoxification.

An article published by healthline.com states, "Some research also suggests that people who eat fish regularly tend to have more grey matter in their brain. Grey matter contains most of the nerve cells that control decision-making, memory and emotion. Overall, fatty fish is an excellent choice for brain health." (End of article)

Amongst other suggestions to increase responses to cognitive therapy are the environment and a loving support team of aware individuals.

It is important to note that change requires genuine commitment and effort from the narcissist. They must be open to self-exploration, taking responsibility for their actions, and making amends when necessary.

While change is possible, it is important to acknowledge that not all narcissists may seek or be receptive to help. The foregoing methods should be explored with some caution to the victims because of the natural nature of narcissism to manipulate. Ensure the progress is genuine and always approach this with the guidance of a professional.

An Important Message to Readers

To all the readers out there, whether you have experienced narcissistic abuse, consider yourself a survivor, or are simply seeking knowledge about narcissism and its impact on our society, I want to leave you with a closing message:

You are not alone. Narcissistic abuse can have profound and lasting effects on individuals, relationships, and communities. It is essential to recognize the signs of narcissism and educate yourselves about this complex issue. By doing so, we can better understand and support those who have been affected by narcissistic abuse.

If you are a victim or survivor of narcissistic abuse, remember that healing is possible. Rebuilding your life and reclaiming your sense of self-worth may take time, but with patience, self-care, and support, you can move forward and thrive.

Seeking professional help from therapists, counsellors, or support groups specializing in narcissistic abuse can provide valuable guidance and assistance on your healing journey. Surround yourself with understanding and compassionate individuals who validate your experiences and provide a safe space for healing.

For those who want to learn more about narcissism and its effects on society, your willingness to educate yourself is commendable. By increasing awareness and understanding, we can collectively work towards prevention, early intervention, and support systems for those affected by narcissistic abuse.

Remember, self-care and self-compassion are vital for everyone, regardless of their experiences. Take the time to nurture your emotional well-being, set boundaries, and prioritize your mental health. Together, we can create a more empathetic and supportive society.

Stay strong, keep learning, and know that there is hope for a brighter future beyond narcissistic abuse.

Message to the Youths

I hope this message finds you well and serves as a reminder of the importance of making informed decisions when it comes to relationships. In a world where everything moves at a rapid pace, it's crucial to take a step back and invest time in knowing yourself before diving into a romantic partnership.

Take the time to discover who you truly are, your desires, goals, and aspirations. Understand what brings you joy, what values you hold dear, and what you envision in a partner. By developing a solid sense of self, you can better navigate the complexities of relationships.

When you meet someone new, resist the temptation to rush into intimacy. Remember that true connections require time to grow and flourish. Take the opportunity to learn about the individual beyond the surface level. Understand their past experiences, their family history, and the values they hold dear. This knowledge will help you evaluate whether you share fundamental beliefs and if your goals align.

It's important to recognize that life is a precious gift, and each decision we make can have a profound impact on our journey. Relationships should enhance your life, not detract from it. Before sharing your body, minds, and soul with someone, ask yourself if this person aligns with your values and supports your personal growth.

Setting clear boundaries is another crucial aspect of building healthy relationships. Know your limits and communicate them effectively. Respect your own needs and ensure they are respected by your partner as well. Boundaries serve as a foundation for mutual understanding, respect, and growth.

In this process, never forget to look in the mirror and love the person you see. Self-love is not selfish, it's a prerequisite for a fulfilling and healthy relationship. When you genuinely appreciate and care for yourself, you will naturally attract a partner who will treat you with the love and respect you deserve.

Remember, you are worthy of the best that life has to offer, and settling for less should never be an option.

Look out for the next edition of "Narcissism Has No Face" for some critical guidance on dating.

A note to **TTNAWH** *members*

As the founder of the Trinidad and Tobago Narcissistic Awareness and Healing for Women (TTNAWH), I want to express my deepest appreciation to each of you. Your belief in me and in the mission of TTNAWH has made all of this possible, and I am profoundly grateful for your trust and support.

It fills my heart with joy to see how you have embraced the awareness of narcissistic abuse and taken on the responsibility of learning and growing alongside me. Together, we have become a beacon of knowledge and empowerment, shining a light on a topic that has long been shrouded in silence and misunderstanding.

To those who have been with me on this transformative journey since its very inception, I extend my heartfelt thanks. Your unwavering commitment and dedication have been a source of inspiration and strength. It is through your collective efforts that we have been able to build TTNAWH into the empowering community it is today.

To those with whom I have the privilege of engaging in regular conversations, I want to express my sincere gratitude. Your support, encouragement, and willingness to share your experiences have enriched my own understanding and deepened our collective knowledge. Your voices and insights are invaluable in our quest for healing and awareness.

To the foundation members of TTNAWH, I dedicate this book to you as a symbol of our shared journey. Your unwavering support, guidance, and collaboration have shaped the very essence of our organization. It is through our collective efforts that we have been able to touch the lives of survivors and create a safe space for healing and growth.

To the members who observe in silence, I want you to know that we see you, we hear you, and we understand. We respect and honour your journey, and we hope that one day you will find the strength to share your voice. Know that when that time comes, we will be here to support you with love and compassion.

At TTNAWH, we are more than an organization, we are a family. We are bound together by love, empathy, and a shared commitment to healing and self-care. I want each and every one of you to always be kind to yourselves, to practice self-compassion and self-love. These words serve as a daily reminder that your well-being matters and that you are deserving of happiness and healing.

Once again, I extend my deepest appreciation to all of my TTNAWH members. Your trust, belief, and dedication have brought us this far, and together, we will continue to make a difference in the lives of survivors. Let us move forward with unity, compassion, and the unwavering determination to create a world where narcissistic abuse is recognized and survivors are empowered.

How have you benefitted?
Reflecting on Personal Growth and Progress

Instructions:

As you reach the end of the book, take a moment to reflect on your personal growth and progress in understanding and healing from narcissistic abuse. Use this worksheet to make notes and answer the following questions. Be honest with yourself and take your time to delve into your feelings and experiences. Remember, this is a tool to help you track your progress and gain insights for your healing journey.

Understanding Narcissism:

I wish you much success on your journey to reclaiming your life or, in helping someone on their journey.

How will you answer?

1. What have you learned about narcissism throughout the book?

2. How has this understanding helped you make sense of your own experiences?

3. Are there any specific traits or behaviors of narcissism that resonate with your personal situation?

Self-Reflection:

1. Reflect on your emotional journey since becoming aware of the narcissistic abuse.

2. How have you grown emotionally and mentally during this time?

3. Have you identified any patterns or beliefs that may have contributed to your vulnerability to narcissistic abuse?

Identifying the Impact:

1. What specific ways has narcissistic abuse affected your self-esteem and self-worth?

2. Have you noticed any lingering effects on your ability to trust others or form healthy relationships?

3. How has your perception of yourself and others changed throughout the healing process?

Breaking Free:

1. What steps have you taken to distance yourself from the narcissistic individual or environment?

2. Have you sought professional help or support groups to aid in your healing process?

3. In what ways have you reclaimed your power and autonomy?

Healing and Growth:

1. Describe any healing practices or coping strategies that have been effective for you.

2. How have you nurtured self-care and self-compassion in your journey?

3. Are there any specific achievements or milestones in your healing that you would like to acknowledge?

Moving Forward:

1. What are your goals for the future in terms of healing and personal growth?

2. How will you ensure that you maintain healthy boundaries and protect yourself from future narcissistic abuse?

3. What support systems or resources will you rely on as you continue your journey?

Conclusion

By completing this worksheet, you have taken an important step in reflecting on your progress and growth in healing from narcissistic abuse. Remember, healing is a process, and it takes time. Be patient with yourself and celebrate the milestones along the way.

While you continue seeking support and practicing self-care, remember the importance of embracing your inner strength as you move forward on your path to a healthier and happier life.

Pay attention to red flags and narcissistic traits as you go along your journey because, "Narcissism Has No Face."

With warm regards,

Susan Sylvester- Barker (Sue Barker)
Author
Founder and President
Trinidad and Tobago Narcissistic Awareness and Healing TTNAWH Foundation

The End

Printed in the United States
by Baker & Taylor Publisher Services